The
China Cup
Approach to
Successful Relationships

The China Cup Approach to Successful Relationships

10 Rules to keep your relationship precious

Alice Vieira, Ph.D.

Take care &
enjoy !
Alice Vieira

For information write:
TPCS Publishers, 660 Baker Street, Suite 229, Costa Mesa, CA 92626 USA

TPCS books may be purchased for educational and business use. For information please write the address listed above.
TPCS Distributors Web site http://www.tpcsdirect.com

Copyright © 2003
First Printing 2003
Printed in the United States of America

Publisher's Cataloging In Publication

Vieira, Alice
The China Cup Approach to Successful Relationships. 1. Self-actualization (Psychology) 2. Self-actualization (Psychology)—Case studies 3. Self-help techniques.

ISBN # 1-885634-05-6

DEDICATION

This book is dedicated to my clients from my Pasadena, California office. As I close that office in Pasadena, a practice I have enjoyed since 1978, I appreciate the thoughts and the insights that have been brought to me by these marvelous people – these hard working, dedicated clients who have trusted me and allowed me to be a part of their lives. Over these past 24 years, many of these clients have grown up, graduated from school, married, had families, established a career, changed careers, buried beloved members of their families, divorced, retired and continued to deal with and solve issues that life presented to them.

My family moved to Pasadena when I was three years old. As an adult, I became first a teacher at and then the principal of Pasadena's Mayfield High School. I began working as a Marriage and Family Therapist in 1969, returning to Pasadena to attend the California School of Professional Psychology, (which is now Alliant University). I began my private practice in Pasadena in 1978. As you can see, I have "been around" Pasadena and "been there for my clients" for many years.

What an honor it is to be in these peoples' books of referrals and for them to allow me to work through their crises, traumas, joys and relationships. This group of people has been my inspiration to write and complete this book – it is really about and for them. My "rules" came out of my work with them –; the phrases I have come to use: China Cup, My Nickel, 70%, Endless Tape, Quirks – all emerged from my work with them.

I would humbly like to express my deepest appreciation to each and every one of these clients. Thank you for the privilege of knowing, working with and learning from every one of you.

ACKNOWLEDGMENTS

Acknowledging the hard work, pain, joy and satisfaction that so many couples have shared with me over the years would hardly express my soul-felt admiration, appreciation and respect. When a couple brings me their hopes for a relationship that is on the brink of disaster, or that is a disappointment to them, I see their souls searching for the hope and the joy that was once in the center of their lives, and I witness their dedication to the effort of regaining it. Although the dedication of this book is to my Pasadena clients, I also want to acknowledge all the clients who have shared their lives with me. To each of you, thank you for your permission to use examples of your struggles in this book.

Laurel Anderson, Elloree Findley, Judie Framan, Nancy Haller, Robert Hindman, Mike McConnell, John Thie and Connie Rubsamen all went "above and beyond" in their efforts to edit, challenge, provide suggestions on content and support the future of this endeavor. I am deeply grateful to each of you.

I also want to thank all of the following colleagues and friends for reading drafts of this book and for giving me input, support, and encouragement: Sheila Burke, Kelly Cording, Stacy Gray, Marco Hernandez, Grace Knight, Jack Koll, Chris Laws, Judy LeMaster, Richard Lietz, Linne Malloy, Pat Nepp, Lynn Reiss, Iris Slonin, Kimber West, Victoria Zarifis and Gertrude Zint. And thank you to Perry Ahern, who did the final edit and to Anthony Melendez, my computer guru .

As Hilary Clinton said, "It takes a village to raise a child." So, too, does it takes a coterie of good friends and colleagues to write a book – at least, in my case it does. The number and quality of people who belong to that coterie gives me great joy.

Last, but certainly not least, I want to acknowledge and express my love and appreciation to my dear husband Kim Vieira, who was with my process and encouraged every step of the way.

Thank you all.

CONTENTS

INTRODUCTION

This book is a compilation of rules and concepts that lead to healthy, nourishing, satisfying, sexy, rewarding, mutually empowering relationships. It is also based on over 30 years of experience providing couple counseling, "disillusionment counseling"[1] and psychotherapy with victims of unhappy, unsatisfying, dysfunctional and/or just plain boring relationships. It is also based on the work I have done with numerous people who are simply not available for healthy relationships. People who have unresolved issues with previous relationships may continue to try to resolve the old issues in new relationships. This repetition is an unfortunate way to not be available for a new, healthy relationship.

I believe relationships are more precious than your most precious items – your diamond ring, an expensive antique, your crystal, and your china. Think about the care you give them. You put them in safe places. If one gets chipped, it is either completely ruined or will need a very special craftsman's process to restore its usefulness and finery.

Think of your relationship in the same way that you think of your precious items. Think about taking these precious items on a picnic or to the beach. You wouldn't. You wouldn't play catch with them or leave them unattended, either.

I have selected one such precious item, a *China Cup,* to represent all such precious items, in an analogy for the care and restoration of relationships. Relationships are both sturdy and fragile, just as a *China Cup* can be restored if cracked, it cannot be restored if smashed to smithereens.

Elloree Findley, a China Restorer, commented: "1) **once a cup is repaired, it is not the same,** it is for decorative use only. The materials used for restoration are very toxic. As for repairs of cup handles, it is very dangerous as the glue can weaken and, give way, then someone has a lap full of hot liquid. 2) Any fine piece of china should not go into the dishwasher. This goes for anything with gold on it. The **sustained heat** and water spray **pressure is very hard** on porcelain. Also, any piece repaired or restored will come apart in the dishwasher. 3) The major obstacle in restoring cups is that, **frequently, they 'spring' when broken**. It is a physics thing. When the circle breaks, one side relaxes and therefore is slightly wider than the other. Usually it is better to chuck the cup. It can be repaired, but the sides have to be filled, which is very difficult to increase the 'tighter' side and end up with a circle again. **It's very labor intensive** and expensive."[2]

Maybe Rhett Butler said it best when, in *Gone With the Wind*, he told Scarlett O'Hara, 'Scarlett, I was never one to patiently pick up broken fragments and glue them together and tell myself that the mended whole was as good as new. What is broken is broken—and I'd rather remember it as it was at its best than mend it and see the broken places as long as I lived. Perhaps, if I were younger—,' he sighed. 'But I'm too old to believe in such sentimentalities as clean slates and starting all over. I'm too old to shoulder the burden of constant lies that go with living in polite disillusionment. I couldn't live with you and lie to you and I certainly couldn't lie to myself....'[3]

The relationship itself should be considered a *China Cup*. Respecting its preciousness is the very best circumstance under which the relationship can grow. Nicking the *China Cup* with blame, harsh words, criticism, derision, sarcasm and defensiveness may leave cracks in it. You may choose to keep the cracked *Cup,* but it will never be the *Cup* it was before the crack.

The idea behind the CHINA CUP APPROACH TO SUCCESSFUL RELATIONSHIPS is that relationships are precious and valuable. Like *China Cups,* relationships need to be taken care of and treasured. With that in mind, here are the "rules" to take care of your *China Cup.*

Collectable China Cups are subject to wear and tear in everyday use. Also, they are vulnerable to surface deterioration and structural damage caused by misuse, accidental knocks and scrapes, and exposure to environmental hazards such as humidity, pollution, and intense heat and light.
-Care and Repair of Everyday Treasures

Chapter 1

ENDLESS TAPE

With couples, I have observed that what each says to one another is not forgotten – especially the bad stuff. I have heard too many times, usually from men: "She told me that if I loved her I would remember to bring her flowers, buy her gifts or have her picture on my desk. I don't seem to do those things, so I guess she was right. I must not love her." I have also heard: "I never thought of her as fat. She talked about her weight so much and asked me so often if I thought she was fat, that I started thinking about it. Now I see her as she sees herself: fat."

What you say matters! *Whatever* you say matters! Some people know this and consider what they say before they say it. I think of the late U.S. President Richard Nixon, who taped horrible, damning conversations; when his world began crashing down around him, he kept the tapes. This is what happens in relationships. What is said is recorded onto an internal endless tape that cannot be erased. Other tapes can be recorded, but once a tape is made, it is permanent.

As with a *China Cup*, words that cannot be taken back are like the surface deterioration caused by misuse and exposure to environmental hazards. In the case of relationships, the misuse and exposure to words that hurt and create pictures that cannot be erased can erode the structure of the partnership itself.

Rule #1
Don't talk your partner out of loving you.

Couples think that they can forget the "little things" that are said, but they don't. Many times things are said carelessly or even intentionally to establish distance when a relationship is progressing too quickly. These careless words are remembered and remain on an endless tape in your partner's mind. Careless, thoughtless remarks can affect a relationship years after the remark was said.

Program good things. Don't program bad things into your partner's mind. You can damage the *China Cup* by exposing it to a series of bad pictures that you draw; they weren't there before you drew them, and neither was the damage before you caused it. It is like each *China Cup's* exposure to environmental hazards such as humidity, pollution and intense heat and light. Words are just as damaging to a relationship.

Irene and Larry have been married for several years. When they were in the uncertainty stage of their dating years, they broke up for a period of 3 months. One evening they each were with different partners and ended up at the same bar at the same time. Irene had had one glass of wine too many and, when Larry asked rather sarcastically how it was going with her new lover, Irene jabbed back, "Well, he is a real stud!" Now that they are married, Larry still wonders if he measures up, and it has affected their closeness from time to time.

Although they are going to be together, Irene gave him a bad picture. Irene has tried to reassure Larry, but there was exposure to wear and tear that was unnecessary. Irene can't fix that. Another example of exposure to hurtful words and how it eventually cracked the *China Cup* occurred with Phil and Willa.

Phil and Willa were dating for several months when She asked him where the relationship was going. He told her that her body shape was not up to his standards, that he preferred more athletic looking shapes. She was devastated and felt inhibited in their lovemaking, and didn't want the lights on when she was undressing. They continued dating off and on and eventually they married. He wondered why she was not more responsive to his sexual advances.

Willa never forgot what Phil had said, even though he told her over and over how attractive she was to him. Lovemaking and experimentation, which Phil had hoped would be a part of their marriage, did not happen. Willa could not forget his remark and never felt completely attractive to Phil. In three years, the marriage ended.

Just as damaging to a relationship are remarks that you make about yourself. The exposure to the environmental hazard of unflattering, demeaning pictures you create about yourself can also put the *China Cup* at risk.

Carrie acted poorly at a party – she got jealous and decided to tell Rick about it right then. It was not pretty! When they got home, he said that he wanted his friends to like her, but when she threw her tantrums, the scenes were hard to erase. She felt bad and got very down on herself. She told Rick the next morning,

"I am horrible. I am an embarrassment to you. You shouldn't be with someone who is so disgusting." Rick reassured her that he loved her and that she was a wonderful woman.

The problem with Carrie's need for reassurance is that now Rick has those thoughts that he didn't have before. Should he think of them at the next party, he will reinforce a thought that is the opposite of what she hoped for. Before her programming he might have thought, "Oh, boy, there she goes again." Now he might think, "She really is an embarrassment. Maybe I shouldn't take her with me to parties."

A better way for her to have gotten her reassurance would have been to go to Rick and say, "I am so lucky to have a husband who loves me even when I go berserk." Then at the party he can think, "She's going berserk, but I do love her."

Richard came home and his opening remark was "You obviously do not love me or you would not have ignored me at the club." Kate was devastated by his comment and tried to defend herself by saying that she did love him and that she didn't see him there, etc.

What her defensiveness programmed for him was that she obviously doesn't love him. What was programmed for her was "Maybe I don't love him."

A better way for Richard to have approached Kate would have been to say, "I was frustrated when I didn't get your attention at the club. I saw you there around noon...." This conveys a nice message: "I enjoy seeing you."

Learn to look for and think about your partner's good side. Look for the positive traits and for the things you fell in love with in the first place. Learn to compliment and appreciate yourself and your partner. Leave those messages on the endless tape in both your heads. Begin sentences with:

"I know you love me, so this kind of behavior is surprising."

"I'm so happy you love this body."

"You are perfect for me."

"You make me so happy that I feel like dancing."

Doug had fallen head over heels in love with Mae. She constantly put herself down, calling herself fat, ugly and lazy, saying "no one likes me at work" and on and on. At first he would reassure her that he saw her as beautiful, that he loved her figure, that she was hard working and delightful. Mae continued to say things like, "Well, only you think that," and "I'm so fat, I hate this body." Then, as time went on, Doug began thinking "If you feel that fat and that awful about your body, why are you ordering pie?"

It was a short time before he could even verbalize his thoughts about the pie. This kind of contemptuous thinking (or saying) is like pouring acid on a relationship. Mae programmed Doug to begin to see her as she saw herself. It would have been better if she had accepted herself and began to see herself as he saw her when he fell in love with her.

What we say to ourselves or to our loved ones or what we hear from our loved ones sticks. If we say that we are fat and ugly, then our subconscious mind programs that we are fat and ugly. If we say that we are beautiful and "slimmer than we appear," then indeed that is what our subconscious mind programs. Think of our thoughts as making an endless tape, and be sure that the thoughts that we think are worthy of the best of us. And what is just as important is that we will behave consistently with how we are perceived. If we are seen as a bitch, a jerk, a loving angel, a sexy babe, etc., we will behave in those ways. If we say we are fat and ugly to our partners, then that is what sticks, and that is what will be on the endless tape

Saying negative things to your partner or negative things about yourself is a sure way of damaging the *China Cup*. Another way to damage the *China Cup* is by telling stories about yourself that should remain in your past or with your therapist!

Rule #1a
Keep secrets!
Do not play true confessions.

There is a difference between having a secret and having parameters around what is and what is not appropriate to share with your partner. It is appropriate to set boundaries and parameters within a relationship.

Know what is OK and what is not OK by knowing what pictures you are painting in the head of someone you are beginning to know and love.

Under no circumstances should you or your partner reveal secrets that are hurtful to each other – especially if it has to do with sex, weight or aging. Affairs should not happen, but if there is one, the partner having the affair needs to bear the burden of it – not unload it onto his or her new partner.

It is hard to open up to someone. It is also normal to want to be completely open about everything, to be known "down to the core" and loved anyway. What you open up, however, the pictures you paint and the images you create remain on the endless tape **forever**. I strongly recommend against true confessions about past relationships or past indiscretions. Let the relationship begin with this new, special person in this new, unique circumstance.

People grow and change and past issues get resolved. Telling someone your deepest and darkest secrets about things of which you are not proud is not a good idea. Parts of you that you experimented with or relationships that enabled you to grow to where you are today do not need to be revisited. Those pictures, which depict a person other than who you are today, remain on the endless tape despite the fact that you have changed.

Carrie was wildly sexual and promiscuous as a teenager. Her boyfriend, Rick, asked her about her past relationships, which consisted mainly of alcohol, drugs and sex. She had since been in therapy, stopped the misuse of drugs, "cleaned up her act" and wanted to get married and have a family. She had not been with another man for over a year when she met Rick. She decided to tell Rick the truth about her past. He seemed fascinated, asking lots of questions, which Carrie answered truthfully and graphically. He told her that he didn't care and was glad she told him. Unfortunately, she had given him the pictures and her words. He could not forget them once the pictures and words were put on the endless tape.

When they go to parties, Rick now wonders who at the party did this or that to her and wants to be told one more time about who, when and what. He wants to know more because the pictures are too traumatic to let them go. The details Carrie gave Rick were unnecessary and did not serve to enhance the relationship. The pictures Carrie created did not break the *China*

Cup, but they did make it vulnerable to surface deterioration and possible structural damage.

Take the Endless Tape Quiz

Here are some questions for you to consider regarding how you are with your own Endless Tapes:

1. In my relationship, have I said anything about my partner that I would not want to have reported on the front page of the New York Times?
2. In my relationship, have I said anything about myself that I would not want my partner to report as a fact about me on the front page of the New York Times?

3. Do I say things that do not foster uplifting images about my partner?

4. Do I say things that do not foster uplifting images about myself to my partner?

5. Have I said things about past relationships that have made my partner uncomfortable?

6. Am I harsh when I talk to my partner?

7. Have I revealed things about my past that were unflattering or damaging?

If you answered "yes" to any of the above questions, you may want to re- read this chapter and reevaluate both the things that you tell your partner and how you talk to your partner. You may be chipping the *China Cup.*

For stubborn stains on vitreous china, put the cup in a basin and pour in enough Coca Cola to cover the stain. Let it sit for an hour. Rinse thoroughly

-Secrets of a Collecting Diva

Chapter 2

QUIRKS

Habits and personality traits are deeply rooted. You've got them, your partner has them, and they probably aren't going to change, so let them be. You are not going to change who your partner is. If quirks are constantly challenged, the relationship will fail. Knowing your partner's quirks is like having a map to your partner's heart. Learn to love, joke and laugh about them together. Knowing your partner's quirks and having them irritate you is one thing that will not take care of the relationship. It is like knowing there are stains on your *China Cup* and hating the *China Cup* for those stains. Knowing your partner's quirks and honoring them is a way of taking care of the relationship. Knowing that there is a stain and accepting it or dealing with it as best you can will preserve the *China Cup*.

Rule #2
Learn to love your partner's quirks
(or at least accept them with humor, adoration or humility).

I find that most couples consist of a "neat-nick" and a "less than tidy" combination; one who folds the towel in half and the other who folds it in thirds; one who puts the toilet roll on with the paper flowing over the top and the other who prefers the paper hanging down from under the roll; one who is always on time and the other who feels time is relative; one who often doesn't feel a meal is complete unless there is a desert and the other who never eats deserts; one who comes from a family who opens presents on Christmas Eve and the other who has never opened packages until "after Santa has come;" one who prefers opening birthday presents whenever and the other who may have a ritual that everyone in his/her family has followed for generations; one who likes salad dressing on the side and the other who cannot imagine a dry salad. These positions are neither right nor wrong; they are the person's quirks. They are preferences. They are differences. They are what make a person unique.

In my marriage, I like to hose down the driveway; my husband prefers to sweep the driveway first. I like to have the dishes washed at night; he prefers to have them done in the morning. He eats salads for lunch or for an entire meal; I think salad is an appetizer. He schedules a lunch break; I rarely stop for lunch.

We are different. My husband jokes that, due to all the water I am using on the driveway, the Colorado Water Department is calling about the sudden drop in water levels at Hoover Dam. I joke with him about how little he eats. We have fun with each other's quirks.

After studying couples for over 20 years, John Gottman[4] wrote *Seven Principals for Making Marriage Work,* and reported that 69% of a couple's arguments are the same arguments that the couple always has. Gottman calls these perpetual problems. I suggest that some of the perpetual problems are quirks that your partner has not accepted. A partner needs to have an interest and delight in knowing these quirks and must totally accept them. Don't expect that they will change. Quirks are part of the person that you fell in love with. They existed before you met, they will exist while you are in the relationship and they will exist after you, should the relationship come to an end. Learn to accept the quirks. If you are lucky, you can learn to love them and find delightful humor in them.

We had a beloved cat, Minnie, for sixteen and a half years. She was with us everywhere we were in the house. She sat with us in the evening. She jumped up on a stool when we were eating and observed us throughout our meal. She slept with us. She loved to be held and touched, and we joyfully obliged her. About a year after she died, we adopted a feral cat, not knowing what "feral" really meant. He was very different from our Minnie. Jack was skittish all the time and didn't like to be held. He rarely came around other than for his meals. His tolerance for us touching him was under 5 minutes a day. His quirks were completely different than what we were used to. We had to adjust and love him for his personality. He was not going to change. We laugh about him now, saying, "There he goes" or "That's it 'till tomorrow."

Personality traits and preferences form our uniqueness and make us the persons who we are. Each of us takes care of ourselves in ways we feel are best for our health and our well-being. Sometimes the ways we choose to manage our health may seem quirky, but we have to do what we feel will be the best for ourselves. It is fascinating to ask your partner, without any preconceived idea or judgment, to explain why he or she chooses to do a particular thing. You might be delighted and surprised at the reason, and you will get to know your partner better!

Samantha and John have been committed for over two years. Over that time, John has come to know the eating quirks of Samantha. She is a vegan and must eat before five in the evening and before seven in the morning. When they travel, John lovingly kids her about these traits, and respects them – making provisions so that this ritual is available for her and arranging his own schedule around it. "I know that you need to have your croissant before seven. Later, would you like to accompany me to the buffet at nine?"

When, as with John, the quirks are respected and taken into account so that both partners are happy, a relationship thrives. Another delightful way to have quirks accepted is to thoroughly enjoy them!

At the coffee shop, Kevin likes to put the salt and pepper shakers back with the cream and sugar containers, lined up with the salt in front. To Annie, this seems obsessive compulsive, but as Kevin moves the salt and pepper back to "their place," Annie laughs. She decided that she can join in the quirk and has begun to put them back before Kevin does. They laugh when she does this and have come to enjoy the quirk together.

Another example of how a husband is delighted with his wife's eccentricities is David and Helen:

David was having a drink with several guests. His wife Helen was held up at the hairdresser. When Helen arrived, she entered the room and "stole the show."

She performed by sharing her adventures. We all were laughing, and I looked over at David. He was thoroughly enjoying Helen. He looked admiringly at her and was joining in the laughter. David spoke up one time and suggested that she relate the story about the time when....

David's absolute delight in her "Auntie Mame" personality allowed and encouraged her to be in the spotlight. David knew Helen and, although she was completely different than he was, appreciated her for the way she could steal the show.
David and Helen's example is in sharp contrast to Jack and Jeannette's:

Jack is a showman – loves to tell jokes, can mimic a gunslinger rapidly twirling an imaginary gun, does a mime act where he walks up the side of a wall, etc. All his friends love it when he gets going. Jeannette hates it and refuses to look at him or even smile. It is obvious she will not support this "showing off." She even apologizes for him. She squeezes the joy out of him and, over time, he has stopped doing "his act."

Jeannette liked less and less of what Jack did, and when he didn't change his behavior (like his showmanship), she felt personally offended. Jack felt like he was losing himself. He told me, "I hardly recognize myself. If I do as Jeannette requires, I don't feel alive. I feel like a puppet." Jeannette shattered her *China Cup*. Jack and Jeannette eventually divorced.
We all come from incredibly diverse upbringings. The DNA, genes, biology, history, family rituals, habits, cultures, goals, dreams, hopes, etc. are all derived from our parents' DNA, genes, biology, history, family rituals, habits, cultures, etc., and

theirs from their parents, and on it goes. It is not at all surprising that we are all so incredibly different. We must be fully aware of all of these differences so that, with that awareness and the total acceptance of the differences, we can form and maintain light-mellow-fun relationships. It is stimulating to a relationship when two people honor their differences and use them constructively.

Learn to share the differences. Discuss them, inquire about them and, most of all, accept and laugh about them. Think about that precious *China Cup*. Do you try to change the little rose buds that line its curves and repaint them into daffodils?

Every marriage, at one time or another, has arguments, disagreements, criticisms, defensiveness and stonewalling.[5] Arguments and disagreements may be a healthy part of a relationship. Sometimes they mean that there is something to argue and disagree about that is important to each partner. Criticism, defensiveness and stonewalling[5] are not good for the relationship. Many times criticism, defensiveness and stonewalling are a consequence of trying to change your partner and not accepting his or her quirks. If and when attacks and/or defensiveness enter the relationship, the damage needs to be repaired. Some of the perpetual issues, such as quirks in the relationship, will never be resolved – and that is OK – but they do need to be regulated in an atmosphere of friendship and deep respect. Gottman calls this moving from gridlock to dialogue.

Ben and Barbara were obsessive about exercising. After their first child, Barbara stopped working out and Ben continued as usual. "He wouldn't get up with the baby because it would mean he wouldn't have energy for his twenty mile bike ride in the morning. He insisted that they hire a nanny to do his "part." Barbara made her needs known but his needs were in conflict with her needs. He made it known that he couldn't be happy without his exercise schedule. Barbara gave in to the

night and morning schedule in exchange for Ben taking
the baby when he got home from work so she could
have some time for herself.

Barbara accepted his quirk to work out every morning. She
made it OK by asking for some time for herself. Like John in the
example before, she provided for this time and space in their
everyday world.

When two people get together and identify the quirks and can
accept them and even joke about them, there will be a happy
relationship. The acceptance of quirks is a basic way of
respecting a person for who he or she is.

Giving Up Quirks Has a Downside.

The phenomenon that is unfortunate is the tendency to react
negatively to having to give up your quirks. I don't think it is a
conscious phenomenon, but it is fairly common. When required
to do so, your partner may give up the quirk because of his/her
love for you – and then unconsciously punish you for making
this necessary.

Carl had a "fetish" for watching fish shows, fish
pictures, aquariums, etc. Jean was uncomfortable with
this quirk. She demanded that he stop his obsession
with fish, and he did. After this denial of his
preference, he began being thoughtless, became more
critical and was less affectionate.

It was as if he had tolerated her, accepting her "quirks" in
exchange for her tolerating his interest in fish. It was an
unwritten contract. A contract she broke when she insisted that
he give up his quirk. Her quirks then became unacceptable.

Quirks are deeply embedded traits that come as part of the package. Think of it as part of the *China Cup*. The cup comes the way it was fired up. The painting is set, the design is set, the shape is set, and the consistency is set. Love the cup the way it is. Choose to care for it the way it is. Pick a cup where you don't want to change the rosebuds to daffodils.

Take the Quirk Tolerance Quiz

Here are some questions to assess your "quirk tolerance":

1. Name 5 of your own quirks.

2. Name 5 of your partner's quirks.

3. Do you accept your partner's quirks?

4. Do you feel your partner accepts your quirks?

5. Do you want to change your partner?

6. Are you critical of your partner?

7. Does your partner want to change you?

8. Is your partner critical of you?

If you answered "no" to questions 3 or 4 or "yes" to any of questions 5 through 8, you may want to re-read this chapter and reconsider the way you are handling your *China Cup*.

Porcelains should only be washed by hand, never in the dishwasher. Put a towel in the bottom of your sink as a cushion to prevent breakage. Use only tepid water and mild soap. Avoid very hot water, as sudden temperature changes could cause the porcelain to crack.

-Secrets of a Collecting Diva

Chapter 3

70% RULE

If you can't get a passing grade of seven out of ten (70%) in meeting your partner's needs, then something is wrong. Possible consequences are:

1- You are going to be unhappy because you feel that the requests are unreasonable

2- Your expectations are not based on your partner but fantasy

3- You are selfish, or

4- You are with the wrong person

Rule #3
Respond positively to your partner's requests 70% of the time.

There are reasonable requests and unreasonable requests in a relationship. There are also issues that are "me issues," "you issues" and "us issues." Individual (you or me) issues, if not recognized as such, can spill over into the "us issues." Everyone has some unresolved issues with his or her parents. Each one of us has problems that we came by over a lifetime. Recognizing which problems belong to us and, therefore, have nothing to do with our partner is an important step in recognizing which requests are reasonable and which requests are unreasonable.

Lauren and Danny met at a party. Danny told her that he was a tri-athlete. She was intrigued, asking him about the event and how he became interested in this kind of activity. As they began to date, Lauren was faced with the time that Danny devoted to training for the triathlon events. She wanted more time with Danny, and thought that if he couldn't spend all of his free time with her, then he was being selfish. Lauren interpreted the time Danny spent training as a rejection of her.

The personalization of Danny's training is Lauren's issue. Lauren is allowing her issue to spill over into their relationship. It is not a relationship issue. If Lauren doesn't want to date a tri-athlete, then she shouldn't date Danny.

Learn early on that not every problem is your doing. This is important because taking issues personally that are not personal creates enormous problems.

Lisa met Jack at a party. He had given her his card, so she called him and subtly asked him out. He agreed to go out, but would call her to confirm. He called 30 minutes before the "tentatively" scheduled time to say that he was tied up but was available tomorrow night. She agreed and he said he would call to confirm. They eventually did go out. She liked him and wanted to pursue the relationship. He continued to make tentative plans; if they saw each other, it was at the last minute.

She felt upset because she didn't believe that he was interested in her or that she was special enough for him to call her in advance.

Clearly, it was his problem. He could not commit – even to a date. He "promised" a date but couldn't be certain. She needed to realize this early on, before they got to the time when she hoped he would ask her to move the relationship forward. These are clearly his issues! Her issue would be if she insisted on letting him not commit to dates or times with her. Their issue would be if they stayed together with her wanting more and him resisting giving her more

Why would either hang in there? The answer is the unresolved issues between them. Like magnets, they were drawn together, not because they are right for each other but because they both are perfect matches for issues that each has from his or her past. The issue regarding Jack's commitment was his issue – having nothing to do with Lisa. The issue of why she would put up with his behavior is her issue – not having anything to do with Jack.

"You" and "me" issues are personal. If they interfere with the "us issues," then requests to change them may seem unreasonable. In many cases, they will have to be considered quirks and then, in effect, be considered unreasonable.

Unreasonable Requests

Some examples of unreasonable requests are:

- Change your religion

- Stop your sport

- Don't read the newspaper

- Don't ride your bike fast

- Hate your parents

- Never see your family

- Love to travel

- Change your looks

- Get a face lift

- Lose weight

- Give up your job

- Stop drinking

- Stop therapy

- Stop working out

- Make more money

- Don't eat meat

These "needs" are too general and deal with issues that should not be a part of the relationship – they are too personal, and if there were a problem with any one of them, it would be a therapeutic issue, not a relationship issue. These types of requests are impinging on the boundaries of a person. Persons who request these kinds of things want to change their partner, not modify behavior. This is not fair to the relationship.

Reasonable Requests

Some examples of reasonable requests are:

- Call if you are going to be late

- Look at me when you are talking to me

- Turn the light off when you leave the room

- Turn the TV down if I have gone to bed

- Check with me before you make plans for us

- Take me out once a week

- Think of places where we can go

- Answer me when I am talking to you

- If you tell me you are going to do something, then follow through or tell me that you aren't going to do it so I can make other arrangements

- Don't stand at the door when you are anxious to leave; ask me what my ETA is and then go do something else
- Start getting ready earlier so that we are not always late

- Stop talking when I ask for a break

These issues are case specific or deal directly with relationship issues. These issues are fixable with thoughtfulness and care. These types of requests don't have to do with quirks – they are preferences.

There are some who have an expectation about what marriage, home and family will be for them, long before they have met their partner.

Unreasonable Expectations

- "I always dreamed that my husband would love to dance and that we would often go dancing together."

- "I always wanted my husband to be the handyman around the house – my father never did a thing."

- "I was sure that my wife would love to cook."

- "My wife would always want to stay home with the kids."

The above are examples of the myth taking over the reality; oftentimes, these same people make these types of things part of the 70%. Your partner may not like to dance or cook, and may not be handy with tools and things. That kind of request, "I want you to be a dancer and love it," is not a reasonable request. "Would you consider taking dance lessons with me because I love to dance?" is a reasonable request.

A reminder about wanting to change your partner: YOU CAN'T, SO DON'T TRY. If you feel you must change your partner in order for the relationship to continue, IT WON'T, BUT you can change YOUR OWN expectations

Learning about your partner and learning about yourself is crucial. The key is to know what your needs, preferences and desires are in order to clearly communicate them to your partner. When you have a preference, need or desire, tell your partner. If you discover what you would prefer as a result of something that your partner does, then use the **4-Step formula** [6] to clearly state what you prefer.

1- **State your perception of what happened.**

2- **State how you felt about it (you cannot use the words YOU or I FELT THAT YOU…. Instead use "I feel or felt angry, hurt, embarrassed, sad, surprised….").**

3- **Look inside and identify how that incident made you feel about the relationship.**

4- **State what you need to have happen or not happen now and in the future.**

Sometimes there is a **Step 5- Compromise to a resolution and a solution.**

The 70% rule is that, when you know what your partner needs, you need to respond positively to those needs. I want to emphasize that 70% is seven out of ten, not ten out of ten. 30% of the time can be a "no" or a compromise ("a settlement of differences where both parties make concessions" *American Heritage Dictionary*, 1969 [7]). The compromise discussions are oftentimes the basis of deepening intimacy and can be rich in teaching you more about your partner. If the answer is not an OK with positive follow-up behavior, then your partner needs to propose a compromise. One person may feel that a request is reasonable while the other feels that it is impossible. Stating what you need by using the 4 steps opens up the relationship for negotiating.

Sid works out of town most of the week. Sally longs for his attention when he is home. There are occasions when Sid must work at home as well. Sally will often ask him to join her at sunset, for a cocktail, to sit and talk "just for a few minutes." This continual interruption makes his work take longer. He used the 4-step formula:

Sid: "When you interrupt me (step 1), I feel irritated (step 2) because I want to relax with you too. It makes me feel like you don't respect me or my work (step 3). What I would prefer is that you let me do my work without interruption, until it is finished (step 4)."

Sally: "I just can't do that (refuses the request). I miss you all week and when you are around I can't think of anything else but things I want to do with you. Having you here but unavailable is just too hard. If you have work to do, maybe you need to go to the office and do it, then come home so we can be together (step 5 - offer of a compromise)."

Sid agreed, even though he prefers working at home and the compromise gets to be put in the 70% category. They reached a compromise that was acceptable to both. If Sid refused the suggestion and couldn't come up with a better one that would satisfy Sally, then it would fall into the 30%.

Disrespect and/or Disregard Cannot Be Part of the 30%

Boundaries and parameters are crucial in a relationship. Basic respect is a parameter that cannot be compromised.

Annie is a financial consultant and works out of her home. Kevin would walk into a session between Annie and her clients and ask her questions or go into the kitchen or TV room, which interrupted her session. She didn't feel respected when he kept doing this after she said that she couldn't have clients in their home if he insisted on this behavior.

Kevin's disregard for Annie's business, privacy and request is blatantly disrespectful. If Kevin believes that he cannot honor Annie's request, then he should talk with her about her request, not act out over it. Every time Kevin would disregard the request and interfere with her clients, Annie would feel irritated and, when the client left, would be furious at him. This type of behavior by Kevin is like sudden temperature changes for the *China Cup* that could cause the porcelain to crack.

Another example of disregarding the safety of the *China Cup* is with Robert's disregard of Rachael:

Robert continued to pinch Rachael's nipples after she told him that it hurt her and was not a turn on. He did not stop. He thought it was fun! She didn't.

This lack of respect cannot be considered part of the 30%. It is deeper than an unmet request – it is disregarding, if not down right rude. Robert's refusal to comply with Rachael's request borders on being hostile. If your partner tells you that something you do hurts him or her, STOP doing it. Ask him or her about it and believe your partner's explanation. You may not ignore your partner's "ouch" and call it part of the 30%.

Be Grateful When You Get What You Ask For

There is an unhealthy myth that if you have to ask for what you need or want then it isn't worth anything or, at least, not enough. This is ridiculous. Only a mother knows what an infant wants – "She is hungry," "He is just tired," "She is wet," etc., and then that is probably only 85% of the time. Adults have so many varied moods, preferences and moments that no one but that person can really know what he or she needs. When you can be clear and ask for roses and your partner gives you roses or a rose, you must be grateful and excited about that being part of the 70%.

Jay and Debbie were having lots of problems and came to see me as a last ditch effort to see if they could work something out or if divorce was certain. They worked on the 4-steps in getting clear about their needs in the relationship. Jay agreed to come home earlier and spend time with Debbie and their kids. During the week between our sessions he did come home earlier. I asked her how it went. She replied, "On a scale of one to ten he gets one and a half."

Jay's motivation to get into the 70% was gone. Jay felt completely defeated. It is essential to recognize and reward behavior that you like, hope for and need. I would have preferred that Debbie say, "He was much better – 8 o'clock is certainly better than 9, but the kids have to be in bed by 8:30, so I would like him to come home by at least 7." Acknowledgment and appreciation or efforts made are crucial.

Take the 70% Rule Quiz

Here are some questions to help focus on the 70% rule:

1. List the requests that your partner has made from you in the past year.

2. List the requests that you have made of your partner in the past year.

3. Have you felt that the requests were reasonable?

4. Have you complied with 70% of the requests?

5. Has your partner complied with 70% of your requests?

6. When you didn't agree with the request or requests, did you suggest a compromise?

7. Do you use the 4-step formula when you state your needs?

If you answered "no" to questions 3-7, you may want to re-read this chapter or ask that your partner read it with you. You may want to discuss your requests of each other and how they feel when they are requested – this is like putting the towel in the bottom of the sink as a cushion to prevent damage to your *China Cup* in the future.

Don't stack china. Store flat pieces, like dishes, with foam sheets
between them. For cups and other pieces, cushion the china with
materials like bubble wrap, foam rubber, towels, or felt.
                                              -Secrets of a Collecting Diva

Chapter 4

SAFE HAVEN

The most positive thing that can be said about a relationship is: "In this relationship, I feel completely safe." This statement encompasses the feeling of being respected, trusted, valued and secure. The concept of safety is essential in any relationship. Think of our *China Cup*. The first thing we think about when we bring the *China* home is where we can keep it out of harm's way – where it will be safe.

Rule #4
Be a partner who creates a safe haven.

I have talked to many couples that want more than anything to have their partner listen to and understand them. Remember that what is said is on an endless tape. Here is the rub – how can you say what you are feeling or talk about your past without putting bad messages on the endless tape? The answer is that your partner has to be safe and you have to use good judgment. Rule #1, "Don't talk your partner out of loving you," means that there are some things you do not share. If you need to talk about your past, talk to a therapist!

Beverly was 38 when she met Tom. Tom was smitten. Beverly told Tom that, although she had had a number of relationships, she had never been in love.

The fact that Beverly had never "been in love" before is information that is not helpful for the relationship. Why share this information? In Beverly and Tom's case, it soured the relationship for Tom. She sounded unsafe for him to pursue her. He wondered what kind of woman could go 38 years and have never fallen in love. He backed off from the pursuit.

How often I hear, "I can't tell him/her anything because he/she will use it against me." That is a clear sign that your partner is not safe, but it also is a sign that perhaps you crossed the line in what you shared. There are things that shouldn't be told to a partner. But if you did believe you had to share something, then your partner needs to guard that sharing with all that is sacred. **Never bring up a sore point or use a vulnerable issue in an argument.** "You are just like your mother" or "You are acting just like your father" should not be used in conversations with your partner. Such statements are unfair, unkind and unsafe.

I often hear the complaint that he/she won't open up. Women probably want their men to open up more often than men, but it is a complaint I hear from both men and women. What does "opening up" mean? It does not mean to drag out everything from your past and hope to be understood, validated and "forgiven." "Opening up" does mean to open up about your present feelings (keeping the endless tape in mind), and to learn about your partner in the present. Women, in particular, yearn to have their partners want to have the same kinds of long conversations that they have with other women. Women report a longing to have their mates be their best friends. Men often don't have those same kinds of relationships with men, and may not need to share their feelings the same way that women do. The concept of "opening up" may be different for each sex. Being a safe partner means that this difference is respected.

Ways to Create a Safe Haven

- Be consistent in your responses. Don't make assumptions or take things personally. Learn to listen carefully and with genuine interest for the intent of the topic, not the way it is delivered or the possible underlying meanings.

- Be quick to be on your partner's side. Don't play devil's advocate. Don't try to help.

- Acknowledge your partner's emotions – don't minimize them.

- Do not take anything personally and become defensive under any circumstances. Take responsibility for a situation and don't blame your partner.

Behaviors That Do Not Create A Safe Haven

- Being defensive

- Delaying discussions without follow through

- Sending indirect messages

- Crossing boundaries – demanding information outside the parameters set by your partner

- Making assumptions about the intent of your partner

- Using feigned compromise as a manipulation

▪   Using shared information against your partner

Peter feels as if he is walking on eggshells with Debbie. He is constantly second-guessing himself to try and please her and to not incur her wrath. One evening, Peter was home alone and heard some kids outside his door. When he opened the door, they ran but had left spray paint graffiti on his door. Later he and Debbie were taking a walk and he saw the kids. He went over to intimidate them, telling them that if they ever did that again he would push their heads through the ground. When he returned to walking with Debbie, she was quiet. After some minutes he said, "You obviously didn't approve of the way I handled that." She said, "You used to do worse than that as a kid." He told her that she did it again, that she turned it against him when he had specifically asked her not to do that. The evening went on coolly and she went home. She called later and told him that since she met him she had TRIED TO CHANGE HIM AND TEACH HIM…. He stopped her and asked her to use the word SHARE instead of CHANGE AND TEACH. She apologized, but the message – that she was trying to change and teach him -stayed on his endless tape.

Peter believed Debbie was unsafe for him to share himself with. He felt "less than sufficient" every time he thought of himself as someone's project that needed mending: "I am a project to be worked on and fixed." He couldn't get that message out of his mind, and he could no longer feel safe sharing his feelings with her. The relationship ended.

Sharon's parents divorced when she was four. She rarely saw her father, and her mother had a series of destructive relationships. Sharon had to fend for herself from the time she was eight or nine. She became a successful businesswoman, and as her career began to reach its zenith, her boyfriend, Bill, wanted them to get married. She explained that she did want to marry him, but that her career had to take precedence over starting a family and, in fact, she was not sure that she ever wanted kids. Bill knew better. "I know that you would be a great mom and would love being at home." The more she tried to tell him how important what she was doing in her career was, the more he badgered her. She stopped trying to explain. He had become an unsafe person with whom to explore her feelings. She withdrew and refused to discuss the topic further. At one point, Bill told her, "OK, we won't have any kids right away" and couldn't understand why this wasn't enough for her to proceed with the marriage. She said that it was clear that he gave in but didn't agree. She believed that her feelings had been dismissed and that she would be coerced to give in. She thought that the first thing he wanted was to get married, at any cost – and then he would want children, at any cost. He was not safe. The giving in was a manipulation, not a compromise.

The wedding was subsequently called off. Sharon felt unsafe to share herself with Bill. He didn't listen to her and he ignored her dreams. He knew his own dreams and was going after them.

To be a safe partner, you need to listen to and hear the message clearly. You don't have to agree, but acknowledging what the other wants or dreams about is crucial to being a safe haven. An example of what Bill could have said is, "I know your dream of being a successful business woman is important to you. I see you are capable of great success. I also know you know my dream of being a father while I am young. Is there any way we can work this out?"

Don't Compromise Too Soon

It is important to compromise, but not to compromise too soon. Think about the consequences of the compromise. By the very definition of compromise ("a settlement of differences where both parties make concessions"[8]), it requires that both parties give some ground. It includes a selfless approach that acknowledges that the solution might not be perfect and it includes both parties. If a compromise isn't OK – really OK – then it won't ultimately work. Having children or not having children is a good example of one of these compromises that should not be made. If you want children and your partner does not, then the relationship is not likely to work. This is too major a decision to compromise.

Too many couples get married when this issue of whether or not to have children has not been resolved. The romantic ideal that your partner will change his/her mind is often a disaster. The partner who made it clear that children were not in the future will most likely not change his/her mind.

Dave and Diane fell in love and decided to get married. Dave made it very clear that he did not want children. Diane was ambivalent, so she let the subject go. After they were married, Diane's biological clock began ticking and she decided that she did want a child.

Dave told her, again, that he did not want children. She continued to ask him to consider having a child. He asked her for a divorce so that she could have a child with someone else.

Too many couples get married with the hope that their partner didn't really mean or will change his/her mind about wanting or not wanting to have children, and may not have been completely honest him/herself about whether or not he/she wanted to have children, which results in a disastrous marriage. When your partner states his/her preferences or parameters about the conditions under which he/she will go forward and you agree, you cannot expect that your partner will be willing to forget that agreement. If you expect that he/she will, then you will be making your partner feel unsafe.

Mary and Ross were dating, and Mary wanted to get married. Ross was hesitant because he expected he would have to move in order to get a promotion in his job. Mary was very close to her family, and he doubted she would support the move. He shared that with her, and she assured him that she would move to the ends of the world to be with him. They got married and Mary became pregnant. The offer of the promotion came and a move was necessary to take it. Mary balked. She wanted to raise her children in this area. Her mother would be available to baby-sit and she didn't want to leave her friends. Ross didn't take the advancement, and resented Mary for this decision (a compromise that was made too soon).

Their marriage ended several years later when he was laid off from the job he had stayed in to please Mary. Ross compromised his career path to please Mary, and resented the decision not to take advantage of the promotion. He resigned himself to the job, but when he was laid off his resentment surfaced. The marriage could not sustain his blaming her for his stifled career. Ross put himself in an unsafe position when he compromised too soon and she became the brunt of his decision. He should have discussed his desire (maybe his need) for his promotion and how he might feel if he didn't take it. Outwardly he gave in too quickly, but inwardly he held it against Mary.

Indirect Messages

Indirect messages are messages that say one thing but hope that you will infer the real message that is left unstated. If you have to be a mind reader to please your partner then the situation is unsafe.

Carole and Bobby were driving when Carole asked, "Are we going to breakfast?" To Carole, this meant "I am ready to eat." Bobby answered her question, "No, I'm still full from last night's dinner." He continued to drive to their destination. When he didn't read her unstated message, she was angry and pouted. He had no idea what he did and was furious at Carole's behavior. Carole pouted and Bobby was furious at being shut out. The day was ruined.

In being so covert, Carole did not create a safe haven for herself. Bobby was at a loss to know what she was upset about. Carole should have directly told Bobby that she was hungry and wanted to stop for breakfast.

Blaming

Blame is defined [9] in the following manner: (as a verb) 1. To hold responsible; accuse. 2. To find fault with; to censure. 3. To place responsibility for something on a person. (As a noun) 1. The responsibility for a fault or error. 2. Censure; condemnation. Blame stresses more (than fault or guilt, which are synonyms) censure arising from something for which one is held liable. **"Blamed" is a euphemism for damned.**

Blaming a partner in a relationship implies incompetence or mal intent – neither of which can, in any way, help build a relationship. The opposite of blame is to assume that your partner is doing the best that he/she can do and that you may, in some way, have contributed to whatever has gone wrong. The following statement introductions will help you to build a partnership that is safe:

"I'm sorry I wasn't clearer…."

"Maybe I misunderstood…."

"I'm sorry that it turned out that way; can I do anything about…."

"It was probably my fault that…."

The absolute knowledge that your partner is doing his/her best or what he/she believes is best is a foundation from which feeling trusted, valued and safe emanates.

Sue and Walt planned to go away for a night. It was their first planned getaway since the birth of their first child, and now their second child was three. Walt wasn't able to find a hotel that they wanted to stay in that would book only one of the weekend nights and they didn't want to stay for two nights. Instead, Walt got reservations in a very nice restaurant. In the middle of dinner Sue blew up and blamed him for not making the one night getaway happen. Walt was furious that she wouldn't make the best of what they had.

Walt obviously didn't talk about his dilemma with Sue before he made a decision to have dinner suffice. The timing of Sue's "ouch" was poor. Sue's assigning blame to Walt makes her unsafe to him. She could have said, "I'm sorry that I didn't think of these plans ahead of time and that I put you under the gun to find something at the last minute. Let's plan our next getaway further in advance." Or, at a time other than that evening, Sue could have used the 4-step approach:

Step 1:   The other night when we weren't able to stay out overnight together,

Step 2:   I noticed I felt disappointed.

Step 3:   It made me feel like we aren't making enough of an effort to get back to our romantic times together.

Step 4:   What I would like is to begin planning another time when we can get away, maybe for a weekend or a single night during the week.

Notice the mention of "we" rather than "you." This type of approach creates a safe haven.

"Let's Talk About This Later" Should Not Mean "Let's Forget It."

As a teenager I would go to a friend's home to hang out. Her father was the permission giver of our activities while I was there. If we asked to go somewhere, he would say "OK" or he would say "We'll see." The "We'll see" meant "No." It is similar to "Can't we talk about this later?" meaning "Can't we just forget about this entirely?" This does not create a safe haven.

"I can't talk about this now" or "I feel overwhelmed; let me take a break" may be accurate descriptions of what is going on. These breaks may be invaluable in achieving better communication. There is an old adage that says "Never go to bed angry," implying that you must talk it out NOW. I disagree with this demand. If you aren't ready to talk, then chances are talking won't be as productive anyway. Oftentimes, when some space is given between the event and the discussion of it, both parties achieve a clearer perspective of the event. If someone is exhausted or distracted because of other pressing issues, this is not a time to talk. It is important to know when you need a break. It is also important to come to know when your partner needs a break as well. Knowing when things can be productive is part of knowing your partner and respecting him/her.

The rule is, however, that if you need a break and ask for one, **it is your responsibility to then bring the subject back up** in a reasonable amount of time. I recommend the discussion must take place within 24 hours.

The partner who called off the discussion needs to return to the subject. "You wanted to talk about the party and I was too tired. Can we talk now?" or "Can we talk at dinner tomorrow?" or "Is this a good time to finish our discussion?" THEN DO IT. If the time is not OK, it must be decided when a good time can be set and a date for that discussion needs to be made. It cannot be put off hoping that the issue will go away. Issues do not disappear. The issue must be resolved or mutually managed, or it will come up again in another form and with resentment.

When a partner asks for time out and then brings the issue back up, he/she has demonstrated that asking for time out is safe. If time out is asked for and then ignored, the asking for time out becomes unsafe and not trustworthy, and the requests will cease to be respected.

What Does Your Partner Need To Have To Resolve The Issue?

Another aspect of creating a safe haven is to know what you and your partner need to hear or know in order to resolve the issue. Defensiveness is never acceptable as part of any discussion. Defensiveness is dangerous and stops the discussion in its tracks.[10] If a partner is defensive, he/she creates no safety for his/her partner. How an issue can be resolved varies depending on the person. I personally need to know that my partner has heard me, that he knows what my point is. That seems to do it for me. Others may need an apology. Some may need action taken. An acknowledgment that your partner isn't going to like what you are doing is better than hoping that your actions won't be noticed. On occasion you might say, "I know you hate having the dishes left in the sink, but I am so late this morning, do you mind?" This comment at least acknowledges that you know what the request has been and that you will not be honoring your partner's preference this time.

Crossing Boundaries

Having boundaries in a relationship helps form and maintain the safe haven. Boundaries often need to be clearly set on many fronts: with friends, with family members, with children and stepchildren and with each other. Charles Whitfield[11] describes healthy and unhealthy boundaries: "Healthy relationships are open, flexible, allow the fulfillment of one another's needs and rights, and support the mental, emotional and spiritual growth of each person. While they are often intimate and close, their intensity has a flexible ebb and flow that respects each member's needs and allows each to grow as individuals... enmeshed or fused relationships are generally *unhealthy*, closed, rigid, and tend to discourage the fulfillment of one another's needs and rights. They tend *not* to support the mental, emotional and spiritual growth of each person. Little or no ebb and flow of closeness and distance is allowed."

When Robert had a girlfriend he would tell his mother about her. His mother never seemed to like his choices in women. Robert fell in love with Angelina and told his mother he was in love with her. His mother didn't like her. When Robert shared with his mother that there was sugar diabetes in Angelina's family, his mother took it upon herself to talk with Angelina about "ruining Robert's life." His mother refused to allow Angelina to attend family functions. Robert had been happy with Angelina until the family pressures got to both of them. Angelina broke up with Robert.

Robert's mother overstepped her bounds and became unsafe for Robert to share personal feelings or relationships with.

A common and difficult problem may arise when a stepparent is involved with stepchildren. Usually, the biological parent feels caught in the middle – between his/her new spouse and the children of the ex-spouse. The fact is that the child is in between the ex- spouse and the new spouse. While the child may not necessarily like or even accept the new spouse, it is the responsibility of the biological parent to set boundaries for the child to respect the new spouse. When this does not happen, the new spouse will feel helpless and unsafe.

Don had recently married Ann, his second wife. Don's son joined them for Christmas Eve and brought a number of presents, mostly for Don or for both of them. Don proceeded to open the presents without regard for Ann, who sat patiently. After the third present, the last present was for Ann, which she opened.

It was Don's responsibility to bring Ann in on the present opening, suggesting that she open one. By ignoring Ann, Don became unsafe to Ann when his son was present. It is the biological parent's responsibility to set the parameters for the behavior of his/her children toward the new spouse in order for the new spouse to feel that he/she has a safe haven in the new marriage with the spouse's children.

Take Responsibility

Any situation may be perceived in many different ways. Unfortunately, assumptions are often made about the intentions of another. Things are often personalized when they are not personal. A safe haven is created when each partner takes responsibility first. When your partner is upset and you listen to the problem, it is lovely if you can say, "I may have said that in the way you heard it and I am sorry; what I meant was..." or "I'm sorry I came across that way; it was not my intention."

Seeking your partner's approval is important. Often, once a relationship is established, pleasing children, parents or friends may take precedence over pleasing your mate. Trying to please your mate first is like taking extra care of your *China Cup*. It assures its long life. It is like storing your *China Cup* in bubble wrap, foam rubber, towels or felt.

Take Your "Safe Haven Quotient" Quiz

Here are some questions to consider in evaluating how safe you are as a partner:

1. Are you a safe partner? (Give a "gut level" quick answer.)

2. Do you follow through when you say you are going to do something?

3. Do you share responsibility when things go wrong?

4. Are your requests reasonable?

5. Do you think about what agreeing to a request means before "just complying" so that you can get through the conflict?

6. Are you direct in your complaints and requests?

7. When you don't have time to discuss an issue and put it off, are you diligent in bringing the subject back up for discussion within 24 hours?

If you answered "no" to any of these questions, you may want to re-read this chapter and reflect on how safe a partner you are. If you don't place your *China Cup* in a safe place, it may get broken.

Collectable cups are subject to wear and tear in everyday use. Also, they are vulnerable to surface deterioration and structural damage caused by misuse, accidental knocks and scrapes, and exposure to environmental hazards such as humidity, pollution, and intense heat and light.
    -Care and Repair of Everyday Treasures

Nicks and even quite large chips can be treated successfully by grinding. When cleaning the chips, do not allow the fractured edges to rub together.
    -The Restorer's Handbook to Ceramics and Glass

Chapter 5

"IT'S MY NICKEL"

Years ago, when telephones came into being, it cost a nickel to make a phone call. When someone made a call and paid a nickel to do so it was a big deal. If the person on the other line wouldn't listen, the person making the call would say, "Hey, this is my nickel." Today, I guess we would have to say, "Hey, this is my 35 cents." Either way, the idea is a very important one. The same is true in keeping a relationship sound and sacred. It is difficult for anyone to confront another about issues that make him or her feel vulnerable, either by raising an issue of dissatisfaction or by simply sharing a part of the day with your partner. It is a matter of respect and consideration to listen – not retort, become defensive, fix or explain the "actual way" something happened. I often hear, "When do I get my nickel?" The answer to that question is **when you bring something up!** Many times a partner will have feelings about an issue but won't have the guts to bring it up. Then, when the issue is finally mentioned, the other partner airs his/her side. This is not fair!

Whoever brings up the issue gets the nickel and also gets to be fully heard.

Rule # 5
The partner who brings up the issue needs to be heard completely before the other partner brings up any issues.

The rule is that when one brings up a subject, he/she gets to be heard from start to finish. It is then the other person's responsibility to be sure they hear what the issue is from his/her partner's perspective. That is the nickel. If the 4 steps (Chapter 3, page 21) are used, then this is the time for Step 5, working at a compromise to get the issue in perspective.

Ideally your partner's issue is news to you. If it is, then you have a clear channel to hear the partner out. If your partner's "stuff" brings up "stuff" you have been storing and haven't had the guts to bring up, you lose! You didn't bring it up so you need to listen and hear the issue. You didn't make the call, so it isn't your nickel!

Mike and Michele have been married for eight years. They fight often. Mike likes to have a clean house, the dishes done before bed, and milk in the refrigerator whenever he wants it. Michele wants to feel appreciated by Mike for all that she does do. A typical conversation goes like this:

Mike: "When I come home and the house is a mess, I feel angry and frustrated. I hate it here."

Michele interrupts: "Don't start that, I have been busy all day and I can't just get ready for your homecoming each day."

And there they go. This conversation is not productive. It reeks of blaming on both sides. Michele could have said, "I'm sorry you feel that way." Mike could have come in and said, "How was your day. You look like you could use some help." They could each take a nickel and get to what is bothering them in a more constructive manner.

Lynn is a quiet woman who has a hard time stating her needs or saying "ouch." She endures and is passive aggressive in getting her way. Her husband, George, is outgoing and states his needs and desires clearly. He can tell her when he is upset with her. When he states his dissatisfaction, she begins to list his failings. It drives him to a fury.

She is not playing fair! When he brings up his issues, whatever they are, it is his time to be heard. She cannot jump on this opportunity to air her list of dissatisfactions.

Sharing your wants, desires and needs in a relationship is hard. Whether or not you are familiar with sharing your needs, it is a difficult thing to do. Letting someone else know what you need or what you want makes you vulnerable. What if your partner says no? What if you are ignored? What if you are belittled or made fun of? Sharing is a risk.

Fanny asked her husband to bring her roses, her favorite flower, once in a while. He would bring her daisies. Fanny asked him to take her to a play for her birthday. He bought tickets for a concert. She concluded that if she asked for anything specifically, it would be that very thing that she would not get.

Fanny stopped asking. They are now divorced.

When your partner opens up to you about something that is bugging him/her, or lets you know about something that he/she needs or hopes for, you should welcome this information as a gift. It is an opportunity to know your partner better, to be able to please your partner or to know how not to bug your partner. If at that time you feel some of your own irritations or desires, then note them and bring them up at another time or after your partner's initial nickel is spent.

As described above, the appropriate steps in airing a complaint are:

Step 1:   **State the situation clearly.**

Step 2:   **State how you feel about it when this happens.**

Step 3:   **State how it affects the relationship.**

Step 4:   **State what you would prefer.**

Step 5:   **If necessary, find a compromise that is acceptable to both.**

Once you have stated what you need or want, your partner has three choices: a) comply, b) flatly refuse or c) offer a compromise. If your partner flatly refuses, it is part of the 30% of the 100%. Remember, in a good relationship, your partner needs to comply with 70% of your reasonable requests. If a compromise is suggested, then negotiations can begin. In a compromise, both partners need to feel satisfied when a final agreement is reached. In the following example, Ann and Kelly do a good job at coming to a compromise:

Ann: "When you stop off to see your friends at the bar after work and stay past sunset time (step 1), I feel neglected and ignored (step 2). I know that you know how much I enjoy ending my day watching the sunset with you, so when you come home well past sunset, this makes me feel that our relationship is not as important as it used to be (step 3). I would like it if you would make it a point to be home for the sunsets (step 4)."

Kelly: "I hear how important this is to you, and it is important to me, too. If I can't make it home, how about if I call you so you won't count on my being there? (Attempt at compromise)"

Ann: "That would be better, because I think part of how I feel is that I am looking forward to it."

Kelly: "I will do that. I also have a request. (His nickel now) When I come home and you are doing your thing (step 1), I think that you are waiting for me to get our hors d'oeuvres and drinks ready and it makes me feel unappreciated (step 2). It doesn't make me want to hurry home (step 3). I would like it if you would have our snack already prepared when I come home (step 4)."

Ann: "I didn't know you felt that way. In fact, I thought you wanted to fix them. But, I can do that. It will actually heighten my anticipation. But if you don't come home early enough, I will be angry – I know how I am."

Kelly: "Let's make a deal that you won't start them until five so that if I get held up and call you won't have already started them."

Ann: "OK."

Nickels can get finished and another begun when the communication is clear. Kelly and Ann did a good job of that. Here is an example where reality makes compromise a necessity. Some requests can be put off for a time.

Jack: "Since the birth of the baby, I never see you anymore. I feel completely neglected. We haven't had sex for weeks. I want my life back! I want my wife back! Could you please set aside some time for us every night – even twenty minutes would be great."

Charlotte: "No. I am so exhausted by the end of the day that the thought of setting aside any other time than to try and get to bed before the baby wakes up again puts me over the top. I just can't and it feels unreasonable for you to even ask. We have a baby! And I am exhausted."

Jack: "This just doesn't work for me. I would never have agreed to have a kid if I thought I would be completely alone all of the time."

Charlotte: "You could help me. You could bathe the baby and get her ready for bed and sit with me while I nurse her. We could be together then and go to bed together."

Jack: "I need sex."

Charlotte: "I need your understanding and support." (Trying to put in her own nickel.)

Jack: "I need sex or I am going to go nuts." (Sticks to his nickel.)

Charlotte: "Please let me think about this and let's talk tomorrow. I know I haven't been there for you. Can

we talk tomorrow?" Jack storms off and Charlotte
cries.

This is actually an example of good communication; not
pleasant, perhaps, but the four steps are there. The compromise is
in abeyance. It is clear what each wants. The jury is still out as to
where this will end. The key here is for Charlotte to bring it up
tomorrow. She needs to respond once she has asked for time to
process his request.

When Charlotte said "No" the first time, Jack refused it. At
that time, the compromise portion began. I didn't hear her
complaining about him not helping her. If she launched into how
he wasn't there for her and how he was lazy, etc., it would have
been launching her nickel onto his. I heard her offering a
compromise that would allow him, if he helped her, to feel less
left out.

What actually happened was:

The next morning Charlotte said that she thought
about what Jack had said and wanted to continue the
conversation when he got home from work. Jack felt
gratified that she brought it up. When he got home
from work, she had her mother there for a few hours.
They went into their bedroom, and she told him that
she wanted to be there for him and, just as
importantly, wanted him to be an integral part of the
family they were creating together. True, she was
exhausted, but she was willing to be there for him if
they could plan out a time each week. Jack accepted, at
the time, but the reality of life with a new baby seemed
clearer as he involved himself more with the baby when
he got home from work. When I asked him if he was

getting enough sex, he replied that he really wasn't, but he knew it would come in time and it didn't seem to have the same urgency that it had before.

This issue was resolved for the present time. If Charlotte has a complaint about Jack, she can now bring it up. It will be her nickel!

Take the "It's My Nickel" Quiz

When your partner brings up an issue, do you:

1. Bring up an issue of your own?

2. Become defensive?

3. Use it as an excuse to tell your partner that he/she does the same thing?

4. Put if off and hope it will go away?

5. Become offended that your partner would dare to bring up something negative?

If you answered "yes" to any of the above questions, you may want to re-read this chapter and change your ways! The wear and tear on the *China Cup* may make it vulnerable to deterioration and fractured edges that may not be repairable.

Clean breaks, with no missing parts, can be glued back together. Where most people go wrong is in choosing the glue. You want something that won't turn brown and show.
-Secrets of a Collecting Diva

Chapter 6

PICKING BONES

It is impossible for your partner to know how you are going to react to something. Many of the things that we do are done "on automatic." I believe that it is a rare thing when someone does something for the sole purpose of annoying someone else or hurting them in any way. We do what we feel is best at the time. If our partner is upset, annoyed or peeved about our actions, we have to be told about it. Any type of criticism is hard to hear – even the so-called constructive criticism. If your approach is such that it feels like criticism, the complaint will go unheeded. In fact, if you or your partner become defensive about anything, that defense, in and of itself, will be the deterrent of any possible change.[12]

In Gottman's book *Seven Principles for Making Marriage Work*,[13] he discusses the "four horsemen of the apocalypse": Criticism, Defensiveness, Stonewalling and Contempt. Any of these methods of handling conflict are like placing the precious *China Cup* in a dishwasher on the scrub cycle or in the garbage disposal.

A major complaint that I often hear is that "he/she won't ever let anything go." The past is always there and ready at any moment to loom up. George Bach[14] wrote a book in the 1960s called *How to Fight Fair.* In it he talked about a partner having a Grab Bag of Gripes. He said it is unfair to reach into the bag and drag out things from the past. The same is true now; it still isn't fair! There will be issues that you both agree to disagree on, but the issues must not constantly be brought up as a weapon. Think of the *China Cup*. If there is a stain in the cup that you have done your best to remove, but it's still there, don't continue to over scrub. Try a different method or let it be.

Rule #6
Let your partner know you are going to make a complaint before you launch it.

My husband and I introduce our complaints with this sentence: "I have a bone to pick with you." The message is that a complaint is coming; it will have a beginning, a middle and an end. It is especially effective when the four steps are used during the "picking of the bone." When one of us is finished stating our complaint, once the bone has been picked, the other one uses another phrase that validates the complaint in a fair fight: "Good bone."

I was at a 50th anniversary party of some dear friends. During the toasting time, both the husband and wife discussed their "bones," and it was hilarious. Chris talked about how Lew would soak his clothes in the bathtub when he got home from a tennis match. Lew talked about how Chris would leave the patio lights on when no one was out there. Lew told of never being able to find their phone book. It was hilarious because we all recognized little bones. When complaints become bones, they can be appreciated as part of the 30% or quirks. The beauty of a bone is that it is clear, it is my issue and I am sharing a dissatisfaction about something that bugs me. It is my issue and there is no blame.

Over the course of time, the phrase "We need to talk…" has met with disrepute. I think this is because the phrase usually indicated the beginning of an argument. A list of complaints would follow, and the "talk" would be endless. It would be a stack of bones! So please remember, a bone is a bone. It is A BONE. It is safe. It is *consider-able.*

John asked Judie if they could talk. Judie immediately put up her defenses. She began to think of all the things that she does for John. How could he be angry with her for anything? These thoughts went through her head before he said a word.

Judie's response is not an unusual one to the phrase "Can we talk?" If John had said, "I have a bone to pick," Judie would have known that John had a specific complaint about an irritation concerning a specific thing. Judie may have simply said, "Go ahead." John could have stated his complaint and they could have moved on. It is safe.

When you say "We need to talk," it is like your mother telling you "Wait until your father comes home…." The wait is worse than the actual happening. Somehow, the "I have a bone to pick with you" is lighter. It isn't "We have to talk." It is, instead, "I am irritated and I need to tell you why" – period.

What John wanted to say was that when Judie told him that she would pick up the clothes at the cleaners and didn't, it irritated him. He would prefer that she tell him if she wouldn't be able to get there so that he would have an opportunity to pick them up if he needed to.

This complaint was a perfectly "good bone," but Judie got defensive and, in her head, had launched into a defense that ended in the following:

"You are always asking me to do this and that (blaming). Don't you think that I have anything better to do than your bidding?" They went to bed angry. Later they discussed that he can't begin with that "We need to talk" phrase. She needed some appreciation for all she did for him (now her nickel).

A "bone" is a way of prefacing an unpleasant subject in a light, non-blaming manner. There are many ways of doing the "bones" – "I have a bone to pick with you" is but one way. In the case of Judie, if John had begun with, "I really appreciate all you do for me. I realize that I always seem to be asking you to do something, and 99% of the time you come through. You really are amazing. I want you to know that I realize that some of my requests are impossible to do, and that's OK, but I would love it if you would tell me if you couldn't do them so that I can make other arrangements. I really did need those slacks, and I should have first asked you if you had the time to pick them up. I will do that in the future." This is an appreciation and also an acknowledgment of her time and as a person.

Another couple says, "Can I have a minute?"

Another couple says, "May I tell you something?"

Whatever works for you, be sure that the bone is a bone and not a stack of bones. Be sure that the bone is placing the responsibility for the irritation where it belongs – in you and not in blaming your partner.

Take the "Bone Picking Meter" Quiz

How is your bone picking meter?

1. Is it OK for your partner to say "ouch"?

2. Do you have a way to announce that an "ouch" is coming?

3. Do you set up an "ouch" with a phrase that you both have agreed upon that makes the "ouch" safe?

4. Have you emptied your bag of gripes?

If you answered "no" to any of the above questions, you may want to re-read this chapter and make an "ouch" OK before the glue becomes too old, too dry or the wrong color to mend the break in your *China Cup*.

A gluing job always starts off well; the trouble comes later - It takes a virtuoso acrobat to glue a broken piece of pottery back together without losing patience and without leaving any unevenness.

-The Restorer's Handbook of Ceramics and Glass

Chapter 7

"THAT'S AN OPTION"

There is something highly rewarding when you feel you can give your input, advice and suggestions and share your experience with your partner. It just feels good. It feels particularly good when your partner finds it valuable or, better yet, follows the advice, which turns out well. BUT here is the deal: Some of the time, your input, advice, suggestions and experience are not welcome!

Rule #7
Always respect your partner's input as an option.

As a loving partner who is receiving the "help," a good response to your helpful partner is "that's an option." And to take it one step further, let it be an option to consider. Have it be one of the ways that you think about this issue.

"An option" is defined[15] as "an act of choosing: choice. The power or right of choosing; freedom to choose." In a relationship, it is essential that the "power to choose" an action by you or your partner is respected. If that action is, in any way, against the power of the relationship, then that very act may be the downfall of the relationship. To mend the *China Cup*, after such a choice, would take a virtuoso.

Peggy and Jim's 25th wedding anniversary was coming up. They both wanted to do something special. Jim found an advertisement suggesting a trip to Catalina. Peggy was not keen on taking a boat ride and being on the small island. It did not seem special to her. Jim began lobbying for the trip, telling Peggy it was a perfect way to celebrate their anniversary. Peggy finally said, "Well, that certainly is one option." Jim backed off.

If Jim had continued to push this idea and Peggy had gone to Catalina, then her right to choose would have been violated. Peggy would have been disregarded and would have "given in." This would not have been enhancing the power of the relationship. Peggy handled it beautifully. Later she gave Jim several other suggestions as to how they might celebrate this occasion. These suggestions were also options.

For the majority of situations, options and how they are decided will most probably fall into the category of the 70% rule. Fortunately, most of the time, partners are just trying to help. If you are the one giving "the help," you can take the response "That's an option" as "Thank you very much and that is enough." If you are the one receiving the "help, " I recommend that you receive the suggestion as a loving gesture, consider it, and tell your partner that it is, indeed, an option. Then move on to the power that is yours: making your decision.

Mandy was telling Joe about her plans to meet a girlfriend for lunch in another town. Joe began telling her how to drive there and what time she should leave, etc. Mandy listened and said, "That's certainly an option." Prior to learning this technique, this would have been an argument between them.

.

Mandy is sharing her plans; Joe is lovingly trying to help. Mandy doesn't want help. Letting Joe hear that his suggestions are an option for her to consider makes it safe for them both.

A better rule might be to not give unsolicited advice. Then, when advice does pop out at you, learn to listen with interest and use the response "That's an option."

Take the Option Quiz

Think about your option for options:

1. Do you know a way to let your partner know that you have heard him/her, that you will consider his/her advice and still feel free to proceed with your own decision?

2. Do you know a way to let your partner know that you respect his/her input?

3. Do you know a way to let your partner know when input is not welcome?

If you answer no to any of the above questions, you may want to re-read this chapter and find a way to do these things. Patience and practice are the keys to preserving your *China Cup*.

Use this method only on hairline cracks in the thinnest eggshell porcelains: Fill a pot with milk. Immerse the porcelain in the milk, making sure the crack is submerged. Bring the milk to a boil. Then lower the heat and simmer gently for half an hour or so. The protein in the milk will fuse the crack.

-Secrets of a Collecting Diva

Chapter 8

"IT'S OVER NOW"

Conflict is a natural occurrence in any relationship of depth. If you are hoping for peace and quiet all of the time in your relationship, you will be disappointed. When a couple comes in to see me and they say with pride, "We never fight," I shudder at what I know will be a long and probably painful adjustment. Many couples try to conceal their disagreements from others outside the home, but behind the walls in their home, happy couples may have conflicts that are discussed and resolved. Why?

Think about it. Think about all of our quirks. It is a miracle that relationships work at all. Bringing two people together, attempting to merge two completely different personalities to operate in a functional manner, with differing viewpoints and different training in handling almost everything, is an awesome, almost impossible task. Yet we do have relationships, they do work and our lives are enriched by them. From time to time, there will be conflict over differences. How these conflicts are handled and how the resolution or regulation of them takes place determines how the relationship will go.

My parents fought a lot of the time. When my father had heard enough from my mother, he would simply say, "Drop it, Mary!" This is not the way to have a subject be over. It is one way of saying the issue is over, at least for one partner, but it is not a way I would recommend.

Given that conflict and disagreements are inevitable, let's look on the positive side. In many instances, conflict and disagreements can be a means of deepening the intimacy in a relationship. Something is important enough to fight about! When we have fine china and choose to use it, it signifies that something special is happening – a special friend visits, a special time occurs, a special event takes place. We expect our guest to honor that cup as well. They need to treat it with the care that we do.   When our *China Cup* has been used it needs to be washed, but it cannot be placed in the dishwasher to be banged around endlessly. We can't keep washing a washed cup.

Gina and Alfred have different ways of operating within their marriage. He is more laid back and she is on top of things all of the time. They go along with their lives, then he forgets to do something or to be somewhere or he doesn't follow through on something. Gina explodes and begins with "You never..." or "You always fail to...." Her credibility is immediately gone. He stops listening and defends himself with statements of "That's not true" or "There you go again, saying always, never...." She recites what seems like an endless list of his faults and neglectful behaviors.

Gina never forgets. Alfred never changes. Gina and Alfred do what I call "Parallel Speak": Parallel Speaking is when each partner is making his/her individual point and neither is listening to the other. The argument itself becomes perpetual and damaging.

Rule #8
When an "ouch" is over,
it must really be over.

The rule is simple. The manner in which a quarrel or conflict concludes is crucial. No one should ever give in against his/her will – compromising too soon will not make for a lasting peace on the issue. If you get "your nickel" and it gets responded to with the 4 steps, then you need to say "It's over now" and mean it! This issue, at this time and place, **needs to be over** so that each of you can move on. This applies even if the issue comes up again in a similar fashion. Ask yourself, is this a quirk? Is this part of the 30%? Have I been clear in stating how I feel, using all of the 4 steps? If you can answer "no" to the latter, then it may be worth stating that "I have an old bone to pick – would it be OK to revisit my feelings on that bone?" When bones are brought up after "it has been over," you need permission or you become unsafe to your partner.

When It Isn't Over

It is not over if one of the partners has been required or allowed to shoulder a burden of blame unjustly. Part of the deepening of intimacy is to search out the cause of why such and such happened. Placing blame may be easier than discovering causes, but it is less effective while being potentially damaging.

Stacy and Greg have many disagreements. Greg usually apologizes immediately for whatever the issue is. He loves Stacy and would do most anything to "make her happy." He doesn't want to fight, but they do have things that come up.

During one session Stacy complained (her nickel) that Greg apologized without exploring the things that she was saying "ouch to" and just wanted to move on. She felt disregarded by his compliance and deference (step 1). It made her feel used and taken for granted (step 2). It made her feel that having a relationship with her was more important than who she was as a person (step 3). She wanted him to understand her complaints by listening and seeing (not necessarily agreeing with) her viewpoint and then addressing that viewpoint, if he insisted on doing it his way (step 4). She wanted him to stop doing those things that he continually apologized for, rather than just apologize endlessly.

Greg was afraid to disagree. He would say OK to this or that whether or not he knew what Stacy meant or whether or not he agreed with her. He would just take all of the blame, and Stacy would continue to blame him.

If you were not given examples, as a child, of how to resolve issues, then it is a natural reaction to just agree with your partner so as to avoid a conflict. Unfortunately, this automatic agreement is not conducive to a resolution. An incident followed this discussion:

Stacy prefers Greg to use the spray nozzle on the hose when he waters. He prefers to use the hose by making a spray with his thumb. She feels that he waters too heavily and the dirt splatters on the patio. All they ever discussed was that there was dirt on the patio and it irritated her. He would apologize immediately, sweep up the dirt and the dance would continue. After their discussion about how she felt when he apologized too quickly, he told her that when he used the spray nozzle the water dripped on his shoes. She asked him to show her how he put the nozzle on the hose. He did and she showed him how she did it so that it wouldn't drip. He was amazed and delighted to be able to please her without getting his shoes wet. Later, they discussed how it is OK to speak up when he doesn't understand something or just disagrees. They also discussed how, when he doesn't want to do it (whatever it is) her way, he will say, "I know you want me to use the ____ but please cut me a bit of slack today because I'm ____." She feels regarded, isn't irritated and no apology is necessary.

"It was over." They were able to become closer as a couple and, although they continue to have conflict (even Greg is taking a nickel now and again), the apologizing is much less and Greg now has a tool for pleasing her and for her to be pleased. Another example is with Debbie and Steve, who have conflicts over Debby's insistence that Steve is someone who he is not.

Debby and Steve have opposite personalities. She is assertive, humorously aggressive at times, hilarious most of the time, unaffected by conflict, willing to challenge and state her needs. Steve is quiet, sensitive, devastated by the thought of conflict and has a dry sense of humor that may even be missed by the careless listener. They often argue over his resistance to be assertive with workmen who do a sloppy job, the paperboy who delivers the paper in the wrong place or Steve's employees, who arrive late or leave early. She thinks that he is being taken advantage of. She believes that, if it continues (they have been married ten years), she will lose respect for him.

This is one of their perpetual issues. The bottom line is that Debby will not change Steve's temperament. The scenario continues:

Steve took a nickel and told Debby that he felt belittled when she kept pushing him to shore up his employees. He did not feel taken advantage of and he wanted to run his business his way. He told her that it didn't bother him when they came in late or left early (step 1 and 2). He said that her pushing him only made him not want to share things with her (step 3). He asked her to stop commenting on his business (step 4). Debby initially agreed. "OK, I won't."
After a bit of time, the subject wasn't over for her; something was still bothering her. She told Steve that she wouldn't talk about his business anymore - that she could see that it was none of her business, but her saying the word "belittled" upset her (step 1). It felt too strong and made her feel like a bad wife (step 2).

Debby didn't get to step 3. Steve interrupted her nickel. It was obviously not over for him either. Their conversation proceeded in the following manner:

Steve: "You are always pushing me to stand up and make waves and 'force the incompetent to be competent' and, and, and. I hate conflict. You know that, but you won't accept that about me (step 1). You make me feel inadequate (step 2). It makes me hate to talk with you (step 3). I want you to leave me alone (step 4)."

Debby: "What should I do when I feel so unsupported, when I feel that things are wrong? I believe that a man should do these things (step 5 – searching for a compromise)."

Steve: "Why should a man have to be the one to do these things? Why should I have to do something I hate to do when you don't mind making waves?"

Their compromise, after many discussions, was that he didn't mind following up on things as long as there wasn't a conflict, at which point he wanted her to follow through by calling the supervisor or whatever the unpleasant thing was. They began working as a team – each using his/her strengths. He jokes when the workmen don't do something, reminding them by saying "Believe me, you don't want to deal with my wife." Debby actually laughs every time, because she knows that they truly don't want to deal with her, and she knows that dealing with him is delightful and pleasant. It works, and she accepts his temperament and appreciates him like he is. He appreciates her for letting him be and for having the temperament to deal effortlessly with the conflict, should it arise.

Some time after this, he asked her if she was OK with all of this. She felt bad that she hadn't let him know that it was fine. She said, "Yes, it is over and has been over since our talk." He then was able to let it go, too.

This final step is crucial for the *China Cup*. When issues of conflict are discussed, it is hard work. Usually, the harder it is to deal with, the longer an issue has been inside festering (not ideal but the way it usually is). Saying "ouch" usually makes us feel vulnerable. It is necessary, then, to let our partner know that our "ouch" is over so that residual anxiety is relieved.

Damage Control

Sometimes, before it is, indeed, over, there needs to be some type of damage control. Angry words are sometimes said; thoughtless gestures are made; inconsiderate actions are taken; mistakes in sharing impinge; selfishness sneaks out. We are all human, and being perfect is not a goal. Doing our best is a goal. When something is done that hurts your partner or is received in a manner that is not intended, then the damage needs to be controlled. Damage control can come in many forms. A kiss to make up is what you might hope for, or it may simply be an acknowledgment that it happened and an apology will suffice. At other times you may need to ask your partner what you can do to make up for what you did. In yet other cases, flowers or a gift may be in order. The point is that to have it be over now, you may have to fix the crack in the *China Cup*.

Take the "Over – Really Over" Quiz

In your relationship, is "over" really "over"?

1. Do you let your partner know when you are satisfied that an argument is over?

2. Do you know when an argument or issue has been resolved?

3. Do you value your gut feelings to know when an argument, disagreement or hurt feelings are, indeed, over?

4. When an argument, disagreement or hurt feelings are resolved, do you take the time and make the effort to do the needed "damage control"?

If you answered "no" to any of these questions, you may want to re-read this chapter and find a way to resolve the feelings that you harbor inside. If you cannot let go of the issue, the argument or the feelings of not being valued, then you may not be able to repair the hairline cracks in your *China Cup*.

To preserve your ceramics' appearance, condition, and value they must be regularly dusted and cleaned. How often you will need to do this depends on whether the pieces are used or displayed.

-Care and Repair of Everyday Treasures

Chapter 9

HONOR EACH OTHER'S EBB AND FLOW

No one can stay close all of the time. We each have a time we need to be by ourselves, on our own. Some people can be together and close for a long time and need space and distance for a short time. Other people have short times they can be together and longer times they need to be distant. Some get distance without upsetting the relationship, while others need a huge blow-up to get distance.

The ebb and flow of a relationship is like the ebb and flow of the ocean tides. The ocean flows in and out on a regular cycle. Weather reports can predict when the tide is in and when the tide will go out. The ebb and flow of the ocean depends on the gravitational forces of the sun and the moon, on the rotation of the earth, on gravity, on the wind and location of storms both near and far.[16] We are, at least, as complicated and as powerful as the ocean. Recognition of and respect for each partner's ebb and flow is essential. The rule is to recognize each other's need for the ebb and flow – without chipping the *China Cup*.

Rule #9
Honor both your own need and your partner's
need for space without violating the space.

I had a friend who was an airline stewardess, and she commented that it was not unusual for couples coming home from Hawaii to have huge squabbles on the plane. (One newly married woman emphatically insisted that her husband eat the peanuts that were delivered with his drink.). When people are on vacation they usually get very close to each other without the stresses and strains of everyday living. When the reality of returning home hits, each (or one) person seems to need to establish their independence before hitting the rigors of daily life. I have met many couples that say they have a miserable time living together, but they are great travel companions. This says to me that on a trip they have enough things to distract them from being together all of the time. We somehow need to reestablish our own identity after too much closeness.

Clara and Matthew both had intimacy issues, each having grown up in families of narcissistic parents. Due to their unusual work schedules, they would see each other Friday night and spend the weekend together. They would have a great time Friday and Saturday, but if they stretched it out into Sunday, a fight would ensue and last all day. It would usually begin with Matthew wanting to "get on with the day" and Clara wanting to read her newspaper from cover to cover. Matthew's quirk, needing to get up and go out, and Clara's quirk, newspaper reading, provided a "perfect" way for each of them to get their distance from the closeness they had experienced on the prior two days.

The way to honor the need for distance is to recognize that "we have really been close, how will we get our respective distances?" A good fight will do. Another healthier way for Clara and Matthew to get their distance and honor the need for that distance is either not to get together until Sunday afternoon or not to get together at all on Sunday. This is a way to both honor the other's quirks and to honor the ebb and flow of the relationship.

Introverts[17] are people who need to charge their batteries by being alone because of their inner world of concepts and ideas. Extroverts are people who need to charge their batteries by being with people because of their focus on the outer world of people and things. Introverts and extroverts differ greatly in their ebb and flow cycles. When an introvert has been with people all day, his/her battery has been depleted. To recharge it, he/she needs to charge up on being alone. When an extrovert has been alone all day, he/she needs to be with people and talk to someone to recharge. If an introvert works with people all day, and comes home to his/her extrovert partner, who has been alone all day, the potential for conflict is great unless each recognizes the needs of the other. The introvert ebb is out until he/she recharges, and the extrovert ebb is out until they reconnect. A good outcome would be that the extrovert says, "I know you need a minute to recharge – why don't you take a shower, read the paper and then we could go for a walk together before dinner?" This respect for his/her process gives distance and allows the flow to begin to return. The promise of the soon-to-be connection allows his/her flow to begin and will not create more distance.

When Intimacy Is Avoided

When we get too close, we may feel suffocated, irritated, unusually critical or "just needing some space." **Conflict** is a way to avoid intimacy when one's capacity for intimacy is strained. **Power struggles** are another way to relieve the stress for an intimacy capacity that is strained. **Compromising too soon**, interestingly enough, is another way. If we aren't ready to compromise or we give too much too soon, we will feel resentful and get some distance within ourselves. **Unreasonable demands** allow for distance. **Promises not kept** guarantee distance.

Val came to me after she and Hank broke up a 3-year relationship. They fought over everything and both agreed that relationships shouldn't be that hard. They kept in touch by phone and both entered individual psychotherapy. Val was aware that she pouted (stonewalled) and that contributed to the escalation of the fight. Hank told her that he felt he needed to be less judgmental and shouldn't react with such intense rage. They decided to give the relationship another chance. For six months, the relationship was going along with respect and civility. Val praised his new approach, and he was thrilled that she learned to say "ouch" in a way he could hear and respond to. When he brought up things (his nickel), she did not withdraw. She reported being very happy in the relationship. Hank brought up marriage and having children. She immediately began thinking of reasons that she shouldn't marry him (intimacy problems). Over the next three weeks, she perceived everything that he did as ridiculous, harsh,

thoughtless and selfish. At one point he said, "Val, you don't like me anymore, do you?"

It is clear that Val was overwhelmed with too much closeness and needed distance. She got it! The *China Cup* almost shattered. When Hank didn't feel he could make her happy anymore because she didn't like him (endless tape), he felt defeated. She obtained her distance by nearly breaking the *China Cup*. In Val's therapy, we discussed how she has never experienced this kind of loving response and the irrational irritation she feels is because it is unfamiliar. She needs to assess her feelings without damaging Hank. If her capacity for intimacy is limited, she needs to know, as a therapeutic issue, that when her capacity is maxed out, she will feel as if she is suffocating. Her job is to recognize that what she says will be on Hank's endless tape. Therefore, should she want to leave the relationship, she can – but it is not OK for her to leave Hank damaged. He should be left in tact.

On the other hand, if it is an intimacy issue on her part, then chipping the *China Cup* is not acceptable. When Val feels suffocated and scared, she wants relief. She feels the need for distance from what feels unfamiliar to her. His loving plans for their future scared her so she distanced herself in the relationship. She could have told him (and ultimately did) that his proposal put her on overload and she reacted inappropriately. She asked him to be patient with her until she got used to being loved and told him that she, indeed, liked (and loved) him (damage control). At this point, if Hank perceives this as her issue, he can accept her apology and tell her "It is over now." They can both bask in their new flow.

When both partners have limited capacities for intimacy because of crippling childhoods with unloving parents, then the need for more space is predictable. The method of getting that space can be enhancing to the relationship or devastating to the relationship. A blatant example is with Patti and Dirk:

Patti and Dirk both had limited capacities for intimacy. When they were getting along, Dirk would tell Patti a joke. She would consistently not get the joke. He would be hurt that she wouldn't laugh.

Each time that Dirk had the urge to tell her a joke would be at the exact time when he had reached his capacity for intimacy. Patti had also reached her capacity for intimacy, and so, somehow, no matter how funny the joke, she couldn't get it. This dynamic would certainly give each of them distance. Each of their ebbs (fading away, declining, diminishing[12]) accomplished a feeling of safety – of familiarity.

Jim and Andrea had a similar pattern of behavior that allowed each of them not to feel too smothered by their potential happiness:

Jim and Andrea would get along for a couple weeks and then they would have the same fight over again. Jim would come home from the gym and say, "Are we ever going to have sex again?" She would tell him that if he would just shower and approach her romantically, she would be interested. She didn't like him to ask her for sex, but wanted him to instead show her with a kiss or some other romantic, loving gesture. He continued to ask or taunt her about it, and he refused to shower before coming to bed.

Although Jim and Andrea achieve the distance that their ebb requires, they are hurting their relationship. They are putting their *China Cup* in danger by not recognizing their individual needs for distance and space.

Another example is of Beverly and Richard:

Richard recently retired. Before his retirement he was a workaholic. Beverly essentially raised the children while he was making their living in a high-powered job. Beverly, an introvert, was used to her alone time when the children were at school. Richard, an extrovert, was used to lots of interaction with people at work. When he retired, she was his sole source of interaction and she was completely drained by him being at home all of the time. The only way that Beverly could get her own space was to have a fight. And fight they did! They came to couple's counseling because they were both miserable.

Richard needed to recognize Beverly's need for space. I suggested that he play golf with someone other than Beverly several days a week. Beverly looked forward to those days when she could have her space. Once Richard got over feeling personally banished and honored her ebb, they were fine.

Distancing from one's partner serves many purposes, from merely needing some space to passive aggressive hostility. For the purposes of this *China Cup* discussion, I will limit distancing to needing space. If we distance ourselves from our partners, it is important to ask ourselves why we are doing that. Do we need some space? It is healthier to just acknowledge that need: "I feel antsy; I think I'll take a walk." It is healthy to acknowledge this need by saying, "This has nothing to do with you, I just feel…"

Be watchful for when the two of you fight or begin to fuss. My husband and I used to have an argument on Sunday nights after we'd had great weekend. Then we began to recognize that we were like the couples coming home from Hawaii. We were creating distance as a result of being so close all weekend. Now we just say, "What shall we fight about Sunday?" We laugh and find the anxiety to fight has been alleviated. Through awareness that we can get distance allows us not to need it. Once "we spit in our own soup, it doesn't taste as good."

Another couple I know plans for time on their own when they travel – "You go to the museum, and I'll go shopping on Tuesday." They make a point of doing this when they are going out on a boat or where they will be in close quarters for long periods of time.

Recognizing and honoring each other's ebb and flow makes distancing techniques less necessary.

Take Your Ebb and Flow Tolerance Quiz

How and what is your ebb and flow?

1. Do you know when you need space?

2. Do you know the signs of when your partner needs space?

3. When your partner needs space, are you willing to give it?

4. When you need space, do you ask for it without needing a fight to get it?

5. Are you able to recognize when a fight was solely for the purpose of getting space?

If you answered "no" to any of these questions, you may want to re-read this chapter and discuss the ebb and flow of your relationship with your partner. How often you need space depends on many factors, so it is important to discuss how often you need to dust and clean the *China Cup*.

Pottery restoration is like any other construction or reconstruction operation: you do not "build your house on the sand," and you do not skimp on any stage of the process, all of them being equally essential. Gluing sometimes involves feats of acrobatics; retouching calls for a degree of skill that might almost be called a state of grace.
-The Restorer's Handbook of Ceramics and Glass

Chapter 10

ENDLESS PROGRESSION

A couple in their middle fifties came to see me about their adult son who was causing tension in their family. They were looking for some guidance on handling the situation. I was impressed with the way they described their life. It was an excellent example of the way couples should look forward to a growing relationship.

Marie began, "We have been empty nesting for the last two years and we are too happy and having too much fun to have it ruined by his immaturity." John said, "We have been looking forward to being together again after raising our family and it is time for our son to have his own life."

Relationships must always be on the upward path, with new goals, new plans, little surprises, new insights about each other and light-hearted joking that tickles the fancy of those things "just between the two of you."
The more couples talk to each other, laugh with each other, and respond to each other's bids for attention, the more their relationship grows and deepens.

Rule #10
Make sure every day of your relationship is better than the day before.

There are two extremes in regard to this rule. One is when a couple begins dating and within weeks (sometimes sooner) they each begin talking about their future. The other extreme is when the progression of a relationship is stunted and plateaus; when the next step in a relationship should be taken and isn't. There are stages every relationship should go through to build a solid foundation for the relationship. When certain stages are missed, it is difficult to have the overall progression of the relationship continue upward. On the other side of this, when a relationship has been established, there are also stages that a relationship goes through that deepens the connection between two people. "You do not build your house on the sand." And, once built, you do not let the house sit unattended.

Susan was meeting various men through Internet dating services. She had a number of dates and narrowed the field down to two; then, after four or five dates, she decided to pursue just one. The next weekend she began spending every weekend with him. They began talking about their future, marriage, whether to have kids, where they should live together, etc. They acted married and they weren't even engaged.

Usually what happens is that the woman will ask where the relationship is going or give an ultimatum about getting engaged. On the other hand, the man is happy with things the way they are and then the relationship will begin to plummet. Even if the couple ultimately does marry, the story of the engagement isn't a happy one – and may even be filled with pain.

On the other end of the spectrum, happy marriages are kept happy by more and more happy memories.

As old fashioned as it may seem, there is a generally normal progression in a healthy relationship. John Gray[18] describes the ideal way to build a lasting relationship. In dating, he says that there are progressive stages: attraction, uncertainty, exclusivity, intimacy and engagement. These stages need to go in order, i.e. after there is an attraction in a relationship, each person needs to get to know the potential partner and wonder about various parts of this person (the stage of uncertainty). Clear observations need to be made: how a person acts, how the person is with his/her family and friends, how they handle your birthday and other holidays, his/her work ethic, their morals, etc. This is the stage of "checking out" each other. If this stage is skipped and, for example, sexual intimacy is the second step, then the uncertainty stage will leave a gap in the relationship. I like to think of it as not waiting for the cement to cure when building a house or the glue to completely dry before using the restored *China Cup*. There will be problems in the foundation of the house or the stability of the *China Cup,* regardless of how beautiful they look from the outside. **Steps cannot be skipped**.

Terry Gorsky [19] describes needing to have companionship (where the event is more important than who you go to the event with), friendship (where the person is more important to be with than what the two of you do) and then intimacy. According to Gorsky, just as with Gray, the steps should be done in that order and none of the steps should be ignored.

Going through the stages of getting to know someone is as important as going through stages of making a committed relationship healthy.

I offer guidelines for dating that also apply to the general rule of making sure that the relationship does not reach a plateau, or worse, head south.

In Dating

There should be no talk of marriage until the question is popped. Dating can and should be romantic. If getting to know each other gets uncomfortable because of real intimacy, then superficial intimacy is the substitute – talking about the future when there is none. Talking about marriage before there is an engagement actually serves as a way to **not be intimate**. It seems innocent at first and fun – **because there is no commitment**. But then it becomes a distancing device when one or the other wants to get engaged and get on with all the – "what has become" – PROMISES. "Demanding to be engaged" puts a damper on what should be one of the most exciting memories of a lifetime. It is not a warm feeling to hear couples talk about how they got engaged when one had to force the issue. Making that moment, when the engagement has begun, a special moment is especially wonderful when it is timely and special. If it is talked about before it is a reality, it is a tease; over time, it becomes a cruel tease. Since our culture still values the man asking the woman to be his bride, it is usually the woman pushing the man to proceed on what becomes a promise to get married. When threats enter the proposition, then the romance gets forgotten. Rule: Marriage may only be discussed after the question is popped. If statements such as "When we get married..." enter an early relationship, the response should be, "That sounds a bit premature." The message must be that it is a privilege to discuss this subject. Speaking of marriage will cost you something. It costs the price of engagement or it will become painful.

When Officially Committed

When a relationship has become committed, there should be an endless progression of newness, surprises, special plans, deeper appreciation, more, more, more. There should never be any talk of divorce or "I wish that I could have..." or "Before we were married" or "I didn't sign up for this" or any other kind of threat to the relationship. It is the opposite of uncommitted. Once committed, loyalty and devotion to the relationship is primary. Apply the rules. "**Honor thy** *China Cup*."

Janet came to see me after her third child in five years was born. She tearfully said that she was wondering if she still loved her husband.

I told her that this was not the time to wonder that. She was exhausted with the three children and I am sure that her husband was as well. The doubt in her mind was not productive and not timely, nor was it effective. She needs to remember the endless tape and use the 4-step approach to state what she needs and to ask for those needs to be met, rather than considering whether or not she loves him.

No Guarantees

What happened to "until death do us part"? Unfortunately, this concept rarely exists and I am not sure that it should. Many couples want a guarantee that "This will never happen again" or that "She/he will always feel…" or that "She/he will always…." Oh, what if that was the case? Unfortunately, or maybe fortunately, that is not the case. There are no guarantees. **We need to do the best we can with every minute of each day. We need to make it better than the last minute. We need tomorrow to be better than today and today better than yesterday.** Remember that looking for guarantees is a way to avoid the intimacy of the moment.

One way to avoid intimacy is to insist that a guarantee exists. "Needing to have a guarantee" is an absolute way to avoid intimacy. The belief that a guarantee is possible is a fantasy. It becomes dangerous to insist that the fantasy is the way life, regardless of who our partner is. This insistence on a fantasy is an avoidance of intimacy with another, and, even more devastatingly, it is an avoidance of intimacy with one's self. A good relationship with one another is one in which the main goal should be to get to know yourself, to know the other person and to be known by them and to be loved as that unique, special person.

It takes time to learn about someone. Part of the endless progression in a relationship is to continue to strive to know your partner – to learn about the intricacies of your partner. Gottman's first principle for making marriage work is to know your partner's love map – to know their likes and dislikes, their preferences, their tender and special parts – to know one more thing each day.

Lisa and Dean read Gottman's *Seven Principles for Making Marriage Work*[20] and have begun answering the questions at the end of the chapters. It became clear that Dean is not sharing his life with Lisa and, therefore, she does not know what he really believes in. She asks him, but he is reluctant to share himself. Whereas she shares her life with him readily, he knows more about her as a result. It was a positive experience for them when he realized that he felt unimportant to her because of his own reluctance to share. He was shutting her out, yet he also felt shut out himself. He opened up and they began having a richer relationship. His comment to me in his last session was, "Knowing about each other is endless, isn't it?"

Yes it is, and the key here is "each other." The endless progression needs to be worked on by both parties or cognitive dissonance may take place. This concept – cognitive dissonance – is the unpleasant psychological state when people hold two conflicting perceptions. If you love and adore your partner, you want to please and delight that person, and they should feel the same way about you. If only one of you is doing the pleasing, it creates a cognitive dissonance, and the partner not doing the pleasing begins to justify why not.

In Dean's case, he didn't share and Lisa did. As a result, he began to find fault with Lisa and to justify why he didn't want to talk with her. Relationships need to be equal in pleasing. The non-pleasing partner needs to justify his/her behavior so that it makes sense. In healthy relationships, as in other relationships, there is a law of equity. The law of equity means that we can expect to get back a similar level of giving. The law of equity states that there needs to be a balance in the connections that we make.

Sandy came to see me after her husband, Joe, told her he never loved her and wanted a divorce. Sandy proudly stated, "I have always done everything for him. He never had to lift a finger. I raised our children, cooked all his meals and washed all his clothes from the day we were married. He didn't even have to get up to change channels on the TV before we had remote control." Between her sobs she asked, "What else can I do?" I told her, "MUCH, MUCH LESS."

Relationships cannot be lopsided.

Redbook conducted a survey (May, 2001) that reported on what is really needed to make a happy marriage. Of the 17 components believed to form the bedrock of a successful marriage, six were identified by more than nine out of ten men and women as "extremely" or "very" important—beating out other factors, such as "good sex" and "successful careers." The six factors were: respect for one another (accept the quirks, and respect your partner's nickel), trust (make a safe haven), honesty (but keep appropriate secrets), communication (pick bones and let your partner know when the quarrel is over), being good parents, and having fun together (endless progression). These components continue to apply today.

Ways to Keep the Relationship Progressing Upward

1. Say "I love you" often.

2. Continue to "light each others fire" in unique and familiar ways.

3. Continue to say nice things such as "please" and "thank you."

4. Seek your partner's approval, not your parents', friends' or employer's. Make your partner your priority. Open doors, think of special gifts, buy flowers.

5. Be on your partner's team and make that a winning team. Continue to try and improve the team by paying attention to each other's strengths.

6. Continue to improve communication with one another. Be honest with your feelings, keeping the endless tape in mind, in a safe haven, respecting the nickels, listening to options, picking bones before they become resentments.

7. Spend more time alone together.
8. See you partner as an ally, a friend, someone who will be there for you.

9. Build and maintain a mutual admiration society between you.

10. Don't accept bad behavior. Say "ouch" in a way that can be heard.

11. Know when it is time to end an argument, and know how to end it by saying it is over or saying what your partner needs to hear or know – be willing to get there.

12. Be a happy partner – grateful, appreciative and keenly observant of the good stuff.

Take care of your relationship. Think of it as the most precious, valuable possession you will ever have. Think of the care of a *China Cup*.

Take the "are you progressing in your relationship" Quiz

Here are some questions to help you consider whether you are "working" on making your relationship grow daily:

1. Do you think of ways of pleasing your partner, on a daily basis?

2. Can you remember the last nice, unsolicited thing that you did for your partner?

3. Do you plan surprises for your partner?

4. Do you "have a laugh" every day?

5. Do you compliment your partner every day?
6. Do you enjoy your time with your partner?

7. Do you enjoy pleasing your partner?

If you answered "No" to any of the above questions, you may want to re-read this chapter and consider that, if you aren't progressing in your relationship, you may be resting on your laurels. This may be the end of the *China Cup*. Be sure that you take care of this most precious item!

In Conclusion:

The *China Cup* Approach for A Successful Relationship's ten rules should be embedded in your consciousness:

Rule #1 Don't talk your partner out of loving you.

Rule #2 Learn to love your partner's quirks (or at least accept them with humor, adoration or humility).

Rule #3 Respond positively to your partner's requests 70% of the time.

Rule #4 Be a safe partner.

Rule #5 The partner who brings up the issue needs to be heard completely before   the other partner brings up any issue.

Rule #6 Let your partner know you are going to make a complaint before you launch it.

Rule #7 Always respect your partner's input as an option.

Rule #8 When an "ouch" is over, it must really be over.

Rule #9 Honor both your own and your partner's need for space without violating that space.

Rule #10 Make sure that every day of your relationship is better than the day before.

These rules are reminders of how to care for the *China Cup* that represents your relationship. In the cupboard behind every *China Cup* should be the directions for how to keep the *Cup* safe, protected and beautiful. Be mindful of what you say to your partner; remember that whatever you say will always be on the endless tape. Respect your partner's nickel. Take your own nickel on your time. Accept your partner's quirks. Create a safe haven. Honor the ebb and flow of your relationship. Pick your bones. Let your partner know when the bone is over. Keep the fire going in the relationship. Have fun together. Follow these guidelines and you will protect your *China Cup*.

Enjoy.

Notes

1. The term "disillusionment counseling" came from a client whose wife was filing for an unwanted divorce. As they had 4 children, the court ordered marital counseling before the dissolution of the marriage. He had planned to be with his wife and children for his entire life. When the judge said "before the dissolution of the marriage," he heard "disillusion of the marriage." For him it was a disillusion rather than a dissolution. I think he was more correct, in the whole scheme of things, and I have used this expression with clients more often than the technical term.
2. Ellorree Findley has been restoring fine china and other precious keepsakes for over a quarter of a century. In reading the book, she wanted me to be accurate in my analogies made to the *China Cup*.
3. Margaret Mitchell, (1936) **Gone With The Wind**, New York: The MacMillan Company. (Thanks to Lynn Reiss and Sheila Burke for discovering this quote).
4. John Gottman, (1999) **The Seven Principles for Making Marriage Work**, New York: Three Rivers Press.
5. ibid.
6. Susan Forward, (1989) **Toxic Parents: Overcoming Their Hurtful Legacy and Reclaiming Your Life**, New York: Bantam Books, and adapted in
7. American Heritage Dictionary of the English Language.
8. ibid.
9. ibid.
10. Alice Vieira, (1994) **Belief Systems and Your Personal Power**, Costa Mesa, California: TPCS Publishers.
11. Charles Whitfield, (1987) **Healing the Child Within**, Deerfield, Florida: Health Communications, Inc.
12. Alice Vieira
13. John Gottman.

14. George Bach, (1969) **How to Fight Fair**, New York: William Morrison & Company.

15. American Heritage Dictionary of the English Language.

16. Sean Collins is the President of **Surf and Forecaster Service in Seal Beach, California**, as well as the most acclaimed Wave Watcher/Analyzer on the West Coast. He is the source for accuracy in my analogy of ebb and flow.

17. Isabel Myers-Briggs, (1982) **Introduction to Type**, Palo Alto, California: Consulting Psychologists Press, Inc.

18. John Gray, (1993) **Men are From Mars, Women are From Venus**, New York: Harper Collins

19. Terry Gorsky's speech to Adult Children of Alcoholics' Conference, **Relationships, Healthy and Unhealthy.**

20. John Gottman.

Recommended Reading

There are a number of books on the market that I recommend today, some of which are classics in the field of relationships:

1- John Gottman's **Seven Principles for Making Marriage Work** (1999) is one of the best books on relationships I have ever come across. I call it the "marriage manual," and recommend it to all people who want a good relationship, married or not.

2- John Gray's **Venus and Mars** (1993) series are good informational books. These offer permission to have traits, quirks, preferences and needs that are unique and should be respected. They also give some specific directions on how to handle dating, forming relationships, having sex and knowing about the opposite sex.

3- For communication skills, I recommend McKay et al **Messages** (1995).

4- don Miguel Ruiz's **The Four Agreements** (2000) is a must to take the pressure off expectations in relationships and with yourself.

5- Crucial to the understanding of the inner workings of a narcissist is Élan Golomb's **Trapped in the Mirror** (1992), subtitled "A child of a narcissist's search for self." The rules in this book will not readily apply to a narcissistic partner. If one or both of the partners are narcissistic, the rules of any kind can be almost insurmountable. Narcissism is an often-used word, yet very misunderstood in its ramifications and ravages in relationships. The discussion of this disorder in relationships is a topic unto itself, yet it is one that I mention to point out some of the traits that are not compatible with a healthy relationship. A narcissist is a two-year old in an adult body. Think of a two year old. The words "mine, me and no" come quickly to mind. A two-year old is entitled to be taken care of, to be focused upon and to have the world revolve around them – they are growing and developing, and the world becomes the two year old's home court. This is the beginning of the battle to separate from parents – to be their own persons. In a child it is both wonderful and certainly the cause for this period of time to be called THE TERRIBLE TWOS. In an adult it is unattractive, damaging and tragic; the narcissist never gets what they want and the partner of one rarely gets their needs met as they are swept aside in the narcissist's need for control. Entitlement is but one trait of a narcissist. It is an absolute knowledge that the space, object or person belongs to and is subject to them. Rape, abuse, control, demand and expectation are signs of entitlement.

Bibliography

Andre', Jean-Michael, (1976) **The Restorer's Handbook of Ceramics and Glass.** New York: Van Nostrand Reinhold Company.

Katz-Schwartz, Judith, (2001) **Protecting Your Collectible Treasures, Secrets of a Collecting Diva.** Woodinvelle, Washington: Martingale & Company

Miller, Judith, (1997) **Care and Repair of Everyday Treasures.** Singapore: Reed International

Index